Karen

and the ..n Sixth Form College
..Road

journalist a

comedy dra

Karen McCa

School, a blac..

Karen McCarthy, editor

bittersweet

Contemporary Black Women's Poetry

First published by The Women's Press Ltd, 1998
A member of the Namara Group
34 Great Sutton Street, London EC1V 0DX

British Library Cataloguing-in-Publication Data
A catalogue record for this book is available from the British Library.

ISBN 0 7043 4607 9

Typeset in Baskerville 10.5/15pt by FSH Ltd, London
Printed and bound in Great Britain by Cox & Wyman Ltd,
Reading, Berkshire

This book is dedicated to my mother, Marie.

Contents

EARTH

FOREST

ELECTRICITY

MOUNTAIN

FIRE

AIR

Introduction

This is an anthology which celebrates black women's poetry across the diaspora, including Britain, America, Canada, Africa, Asia and the Caribbean. The voices, forms and themes are many and distinct: what links them is the shared experience of being black – in all its many combinations – and being women, a shared history and a shared reality that transcend physical and geographical boundaries.

This book is structured around the idea that younger generations of poets are co-existing with established writers, the roots and influence of what has gone before is drawn upon, and from that fusion a different, contemporary voice is emerging, which expresses a multitude of concerns, old and new. Black poets are experimenting with form and medium: they are producing dramatisations in verse, and albums and CDs – such as Akure Wall's experimental *Afromorph Text*, which stretches the generic elastic between text and music, voice and sound; they are collaborating with visual artists and musicians; they are pushing the boundaries between poetry and performance art – performing in 'non-traditional' venues like night clubs and at 'digital slams' with instantaneous trans-global 'call and response,' in spoken word pop groups; and they are producing videos and publishing on the Internet.

But performance is only part of the picture. Black women poets are also actively working towards the creation of a new literature, and the establishment of a critical context from which to assess it. They are producing extended narrative works, such as Bernardine Evaristo's novel in verse *Lara*, running ongoing writers' groups and organising debates and conferences to explore the development and status of the art form. In the United States black women's contemporary poetry has a longer tradition to draw upon and is already at the heart of the 'established literary canon' – Maya Angelou wrote the historic poem *On the Pulse of the Morning* for the inauguration of President Clinton, Alice Walker and Rita Dove have won the prestigious Pulitzer Prize and Rita Dove was also the Poet Laureate of the United States from 1993 to 1995.

However, whatever the form or the medium, the poet is dealing with the word as expression of experience – and this is the guiding maxim which I tried to keep in mind while selecting poems for *Bittersweet*. Thus, any poem, whatever the intended outlet, should work in a written form, even if there are additional composite parts which support and embellish a piece; if it is a poem, then the words – and their metre, rhythm and arrangement – are the discipline, the backbone, the architecture.

In compiling *Bittersweet* I had a huge resource of writers to draw upon from all over the world, so while I wanted to try and be as broadly representative in as many ways as possible, and choose poems on the arguably dubious basis that I simply 'liked them', I felt the anthology needed the focus of some thematic outline. At the same time, I didn't want theme to be a limiting construct, so rather than focusing on one specific topic, I decided to hang the poems around the notion of womanhood – and I don't have any fixed definition of what I mean by that – and see where it led. Thus, the book takes the reader through the different stages and tangents of women's lives: chronologically, from the innocent pleasures and the pain of childhood; emotionally, as we bask in the sunshine and burn in the rays of love; politically, as words become our swords; and spiritually, through, full circle, to the acceptance of our own, and our loved ones' mortality.

Certainly, the breadth of work included in this anthology is not definitive, but it does, I hope, go some way towards demonstrating the sheer range of poetry that is out there, in terms of form, content and author. Thus the writings of poets like Alice Walker, Nikki Giovanni and Pat Parker, all of whose work is highly politicised and has inspired generations of women, stand beside the evocative documentary of Chitra Banarjee Divakaruni, the delicacy of Sujata Bhatt, the understated discipline of Olive Senior, and the lyrical intensity of Dionne Brand. I have also had the pleasure of being able to provide a showcase for some new, and in some cases previously unpublished, talents, like Janet Kofi-Tsekpo, whose work displays a raw and impassioned elegance, Trinidadian powerhouse Melvina Hazard, and the wry musings of Hope Massiah.

For me personally, the poem is an expression of spirit, feeling and emotion – not a rambling, undisciplined outburst, but the distillation of an experience suspended in time. And, inevitably, like life, those experiences and emotions can be sweet and they can be bitter. If, as Lorna Goodison puts it, 'some of [our] worst wounds have healed into poems' then poems are the scars of our experience – the fine silver scars of creativity expressed, the scars we can be proud to show.

Karen McCarthy

water

Janet Kofi-Tsekpo

Birthplace

(For my mother)

Souls grieve into human form.
Morning milks my night,
is sucking on a dream of

love so cold it burns. In a
dark place where the air
is still, eyes pocket thoughts like

crystals hidden in the hot
earth. Light fingers unspoken
skin, relentless, regardless,

memory undressed
under a bald day.
Ocean FM is

pouring soul out of plastic –
young shebas screaming
'baby love' – as gulls

surf the horizon looking
for a soft catch. I
never left this island, but

carried it with me –
this fearful child with
no knowledge of origins;

no memory of palm trees,
hairy mammoths, wild cats, its
pirate civilisation

borne of a muddied harbour,
now contained in the cellar
of the district one museum.

You worked in the library
and, barefoot, took me
in your belly to the depths

of that submerged world –
a singing fish, lost to gulls' cries
and ships at anchor,

rebirthing yourself
beyond the broken walls
of an English seaside town.

You stood at this window once,
bawling like a lost siren,
laden with the vessel of

a helpless body,
as I milked your longing with
fresh gums, claiming your

4

life as my own. I have come
to let go. But still,
something rolls up inside me

like a terrific secret,
squeezes through the tunnel of
those years, and as the

ocean unravels its tongue
to speak, I can hear our souls
breathing on the wintry shore.

Ntozake Shange

Oh, I'm 10 Months Pregnant

i tried to tell the doctor
i really tried to tell her
tween the urine test & the internal exam/
when her fingers were circling my swollen cervix
i tried
to tell her the baby was confused
the baby doesnt know
she's not another poem

you see/i was working on a major piece of fiction
at the time of conception
'doctor/are you listening?'
had just sent 4 poems off to the *new yorker*
& was copy-editing a collection of plays
during those 'formative first twelve weeks'
there were numerous opening parties
all of which involved me & altered the poor baby's
amniotic bliss/
    'doctor/the baby doesn't think she shd
    come out that way!'

i mean/she thinks she shd come up/not down
into the ground/she thinks her mother made up things
nice things ugly things but made up things nonetheless
unprovable irrational subjective fantastic things
not subject to objective or clinical investigation/
she believes the uterine cave is a metaphor
        'doctor/you have to help me'

this baby wants to jump out of my mouth
at a reading someplace/
the baby's refusing to come out/down
she wants to come out a spoken word
& i have no way to reach her/she is
no mere choice of words/how can i convince her
to drop her head & take on the world like the rest of us
she cant move up till she comes out
        'whatever shall i do? I've been pregnant
        a long time'

i finally figured out what to say
to this literary die-hard of a child of mine
'you are an imperative my dear'/& i felt her startle
toward my left ovary then i said/'as an imperative
it is incumbent upon you to present yrself'

Ramabai Espinet

Afterbirth

After the birth
I huddled into my leftover skin
Cold, alone.
Bewildered
But swathed in light
My shell-reality intact,
Distant, removed
Objectified.

A soft unshelled
Mollusc mass
I lay on the table
Trembling and afraid
But sisters brought hot sheets
Lowered the narrow ledge
On which I perched
Helped me to safety.

Some cradled the new life
Some held me
Some murmured and soothed

And all lent strength.
When we move in love
Not war
When our linked arms around
The globe create peace
When we fasten our bellies
To the guns of our sons
And stop the waste,
I shall remember this:
The day I quivered and sought shelter
The day my sister wrapped
And kept me and my newborn
Warm.

Jamika Ajalon

For Jean W.

She grabbed the moon
to her belly
from her navel
an umbilical runway
she birthed the SKY

blood

At Age 4

at
age 4
little girls
shouldnt have
to deal with the
bloodied residue
of a torn hymen
or feel the need
to reconstruct
a broken
spirit

Amiti Grech

Boat Ride

The boat,
hollowed tree
with bamboo hoods,
a floating house.
Under one hood
boiled the cooking pot;
the other covered our bed.

So we glided up-river.
Kaka was the man
with the gun.
We passed paddy fields,
banks of watermelons,
then came to a copse
where trees wore flocks
of green pigeons.
Silence, silence, children,
With finger on lip
Kaka leapt
from the boat.
The boys followed,
but I was told
to stay.

Water echoed
the thud of shots.
I rushed to see the spoil,
disobeyed Father.

Birds, green birds,
with still wings
strung on a pole,
no more flashing
the green of the jungle.

My feet slipped,
I slithered neck-deep
into the river,
and was dragged
a rag-doll
most misshapen,
and gently reprimanded
by Father.
I shook
with fear of near-death,
I spread my wet hair
like feathers.

Chitra Banarjee Divakaruni

The *Nishi*

I

Sometimes I wake up suddenly with the blood hammering in my chest and hear it, a voice I can't quite place, deep inside the tunnel of my ear, tiny, calling my name, pulling out the syllables like threads of spun-sugar, *Chit-ra, Chit-ra.*

II

When I was very little, my mother used to sing me to sleep. Or tell me stories. A jewel was stitched to the end of each, and when her voice reached that place, it took on a shivering, like moonlit water.

III

Some nights I woke to hear her through the thin bedroom wall. *Not tonight, please, not tonight.* Shuffles, thuds, panting, then a sharp cry, like a caught bird's. I would burrow into the pillow that smelled of stale lint and hair oil, squinch shut my eyes so red slashes appeared, hold my breath till all I heard was the roaring in my ears.

IV

After father left her she rarely spoke above a whisper. *Go to the closet under the stairs*, she would say, very soft. *I don't want to see your face.* Her voice was a black well. If I fell into it, I would never find my way out. So the closet, with its dry, raspy sounds, a light papery feel like fingers brushing against my leg, making me pee in my pants.

V

What do you do when the dark presses against your mouth, a huge clammy hand to stop you crying? What do you do when the voice has filled the insides of your skull like a soaked sponge?

VI

Late at night she would come and get me, pick up my dazed body and hug me to her, pee and all. *I'm sorry, baby, so sorry, so sorry.* Feather kisses down the tracks of dried tears. But perhaps I am dreaming this. Even in the dream she doesn't say *This won't ever happen again.*

VII

I will never have children. Because I have no dark closets in my house, because I don't sing, because I cannot remember any of my mother's stories. Except one.

VIII

That night she took out the harmonium, the first time since father left. It was covered in cobwebs, but she didn't dust them away. They clung to her fingers as she played. She let me stay and

17

listen. Outside, a storm. When the thunder came, she let me hide my face in her lap. She was singing love songs. She sang for hours, till her voice cracked. Then she told me the tale of the *Nishi*. She held me till I slept, and when she put me to bed, she locked me in. It was an act of kindness, I think, so I would not be the first to discover her body hanging from the ceiling of the bedroom that was now hers alone.

IX

The Nishi, said my mother, *are the spirits of those who die violent deaths. They come to you at night and call your name in the voice you love most. But you must never answer them, for if you do, they suck away your soul.*

X

Sometimes I wake up, blood hammering, hear it, a voice, deep inside a tunnel, tiny, pulling out the syllables, *Chit-ra, Chit-ra.* I squinch shut my eyes and answer, calling her back, wanting to be taken. But when I open them I am still here, webbed in by the sound of her name, its unbearable sweetness, its unbreakable threads of spun-sugar.

Allison Joseph

On Sidewalks, On Streetcorners, As Girls

Just who was Miss Mary Mack,
all dressed in black, with her stalwart buttons
up and down her back, her patient request
for fifty cents to see some bedraggled circus elephant
jump a fence? As children, we never asked
who she was, content instead to clap out her story
in pairs, our hands meeting, then parting
in quick motions. When we sang
We're going to Kentucky, we're going to the Fair,
to see the señorita with flowers in her hair,
we'd shake our little girl hips in time
with the melody, but we never stopped to ask
what a lovely *señorita* was doing at a fair,
and we possessed no knowledge of where
Kentucky was, didn't even know
what one did at a fair – children who only
knew cinderblock and cement,
corner storefronts, brick high-rises.
We sang about Miss Lucy
and her prized steamboat,
the steamboat destined for heaven

and Miss Lucy for hell;
sang *rumble to the bottom,*
rumble to the top,
one girl in the midst of the circle
twirling and twirling until she stopped,
finger pointed at the next girl
who would shake her stuff in front
of us, our chants heard in every
schoolyard, every parking lot,
everywhere small dark girls
could gather to hear their voices swell
in nonsense rhyme, neighborhood chant.
Hands and feet would stomp out rhythms
inherited from older sisters – story-songs
about seeing London, seeing France.
sassy songs about someone's mama
doing wrong, acting crazy.
No one would dare take away
our homemade streetcorner music,
so we'd spend every afternoon after school
and every shred of summer daylight
riffing, scatting, improvising,
unafraid to tell each other
shake it to the east,
shake it to the west,
shake it to the one
you love the best.

Dorothea Smartt

forget

convenient forgetfulness is my guard
against slights and hurts
your vacant this-isn't-happening eyes
I don't remember a lot of things
quite deliberately shoving it away inside me
imploding later when I least expect it
I don't remember why should I
walk with it hold it know it
for all its unpleasantness feel it
choke me smoke me dope me
I don't remember is
my favourite reply when put on the spot
about how I got broken that time
I don't remember the sound
the impact of your words shattering me
as you chatted on dismissing a quiet plea
saying again don't be boring shuddering
as another piece hit the playground tarmac
spreading into a pool of once-me
trampled again and again
by my big sister's silences and refusals
to look me in the eye at least

to share a silent moment of sympathy
I don't remember my wanting you
to do the enid blyton best friend thing
and rescue me from the little girls that bullied me
or you bringing the taunting to our front-room
laughing at my swan neck and my cowardy-custard ways
only the mirage of my hopeful fantasy
of ever-lasting super-glue love
like the infant fingers of that boy in my class
doing eveything together
grown like one like twin plantains
that could never be parted with whole skin
that would not re-member itself
always being in half
I don't remember being unwanted
the day I ran out the school gate
away from the isolation of everybody else's eyes
witnessing another humiliation
out the school gate to get away from – who
I don't remember
Mr Grant with his big six-foot army self
charging after me escorting me
an easy captive in biting April sleet
white as his big hand
leading up to the hair in his nose
a crowd of schoolkids telling me
I was really in trouble now
and the only eyes I wanted to see me were yours
away over at the other end of the playground

you wouldn't see me there
walking home I could never tell
feeling too shame in your don't care eyes
convenient forgetfulness stinging
from your mouth to the soothing front-door
of our Yelverton Road home
where you were all the world I thought I needed

Learning to Dance

A month before the Senior Social
at the Boys' School, we girls
who didn't know how to dance
were herded into the music hall that smelled
of old dust. Under the glinty horn-rimmed eye
of Sister Mercedes, we practiced
polka and fox-trot, while from behind the moldy curtains
our Anglo-Indian classmates
sniggered. How we envied

their short curled hair, their names
that dropped cleanly off the nuns' lips:
Diane, Melinda, Margaret. *Our* hair hung
limp-braided down our backs
like our mothers', tamed by generations
of coconut oil. Our names,
Malabika, Basudha, Chandra,
tangled as wild vines, caught
on the frustrated tongues of our teachers
until they spat them out. Brought up
on tabla and sitar instead of Elvis, we knew
we were the disgrace of the school. And so

we practiced the cha-cha-cha
as though our lives depended on it. Foreheads
creased, we tried to remember which partner
was the 'man' and who
was the 'woman,' as Sister beat steely time
with a ruler against her palm. *Thwack*-two-three,
thwack-two-three, and we waltzed
over a worn-wood floor marked with large X's
to make us keep our places. Lost souls in limbo, we stumbled
backward over heels, knocked knee
against knobby girl-knee, while Sister rapped out
The Blue Danube. A damp light

fell through the thick panes
onto our sallow faces, and Sister's voice
boomed down from the high slanted ceiling like God's,
Not so close, not so CLOSE, making us
jump and lose count. We were to keep
twelve inches between us
and the bodies of boys at all times
or the unthinkable might occur. We knew

this was true, from the veiled warnings
dropped in Moral Science class
by hairy-lipped Sister Baptista, from the *True Love*
comic books we read under night-blankets
by flashlight. We knew it from holidays at home,
our mothers' low-voiced conversations which stopped
when we entered the room. Boys' bodies,

smelling of hockey, male soap; residual blood
from torn knees and elbows.
The thought filled our mouths
with the wet metal taste of fear
or lust. Even in that Darjeeling air, cold
as the breath of icebergs, sweat sprouted
between our clamped palms, our guilty fingers
left moist streaks on the white blouses
of our dancing partners. For years

we had watched from dark dormitory windows
the Senior girls filing into the bus
that gleamed yellow as a warning through the night
Long after they left, we smelled their perfume
in the hollows of our bodies. Their starched ruffles
scratched *our* throats, *our* breasts. We heard again
the bus start with a roar, headlights
outlining needles of rain, tail-lights like
smudged drops of blood
receding into blackness. We lay sleepless,

thinking of the slight tremble of boy-hands,
stubbed nails, lips fuzzy with new moustaches. The dance floor
opened like petals, the music was a wave
in which we drown. We tossed as in fever until
we heard them return,
giggles and whispered secrets, the spent triumphant odor
of sweat and hair spray. Now that moment
was ours – or would be, if only
we could learn to tango. So

we practiced side-steps on aching toes
and prayed for a Cinderella nimbleness, we
closed our eyes and believed in the sparkling arms
of princes, one for each of us. We sway-circled
the room, around, around, each ring
drawing us tighter toward the center,
that rain-lit night when all secrets
would be revealed, we held our breaths
until Sister's voice disappeared
under the red roar in our ears, we whirled
to the future on our blood beat.

Safiya Henderson-Holmes

a girl and her doll

whatya want outta me?
i'm not coming outta the closet.
you people don't make it
easy. i'm thirteen. she's older,
neat, clean, pretty. i just,
i don't know, just want
to hold her, hold a woman
without being called a weird
name. without going home
all beat up. like what do you
want me to say, say i'm a demon
child, say i'm drugged
are those pains better. no.
i go with barbie. not like
the other girls, or the boys.
i just go with her real quiet.
in my room. i got nothin
but barbie stuff. i like
her clothes. her hair.
i don't know, i just be
with her. normal for me.

and barbie to be in the closet
together, we're kind of like
the same. lonely girls
with too many people
pointing at us. barbie's
are the first girl lips
i've claimed as mine.
so what's all this, you gonna
write about me and her, or
what?

Bernardine Evaristo

An abridged excerpt from *Lara*

Lara is an epic verse novel which traces the two ancestral strands of Lara, the spirited daughter of a Nigerian father and British mother who grows up in surburban London in the 60s and 70s. It travels from nineteenth-century Brazil to colonial Lagos, from Ireland at the turn of the century to Little Italy in Islington. Told through the multiple poetic voices of her ancestors, friends, family and Lara herself, these strands of history finally come together when she travels down the Amazon river in the 90s.
This extract looks at the way in which Lara's identity is shaped by her background.

Lara's skin oozed honey in late summer's oven
lounging amid triffid grass where dandelions fainted
diseased apples were decimated by maggots; wasps
sucked the sugar of bleeding cherries; she langorously
gorged purple flesh, her lips stained Midnight Mauve
Lara's sepia cheeks rouged with the heat of summer.
Sunken on a ripped deck chair, she bathed, tired
of the school holidays, six weeks down, two to go
What was the sea like, she wondered, 'All blue and grey.'
Edith told her, 'But the beach makes your toes messy.'
Full on to the sun, its strokes painted her a rusty brown
until sun-drunk, she stumbled inside, 'Look, I've a sun tan!'

'Don't be silly, dear.' Ellen mumbled, rolling thick pastry.
Three at a time, she vaulted the stairs, passing Fabian,
'Jagger-lips!' he teased, sliding down the bannisters,
out of her reach 'Watusi-head,' she retaliated loudly,
reaching her attic bedroom and slamming the door.
She studied her lips in the mirror, they weren't too big,
not like her father's or that Nat King Cole man
whose boring Mona Lisa drifted up the stairs at night.
Still, she'd suck them in from now on, just in case.

Tank tops, Curly Wurlys, blue mascara, Top 20,
T.Rex, Jackson 5, Bowie, Slade, the Sweet, the 70s
spun Lara into the kaleidoscope of teeny bop,
at Eltham Hill Girls she torpedoed chewing gum
on entering, hitched her skirt on exiting, tissue-padded
her non-existents in the upstairs loo, and choked
over smoke at lunchtime behind the Jubilee Gardens.
Lacrosse, rounders, tennis, hockey, swimming, relay
rotated weekly with maths, physics, history, Latin et al,
 ad infinitum, timetabled to inject seeds of academia
into hormonal cells. Lara, now La and Susie, aka Soos,
blooded a pin-prick bond forged on a passion for boys,
pop, clothes and garrulous babble. Shorn playing fields
lolled from tennis courts to the slopes of Eltham Green,
stunted herbaceous borders prettified the red-brick
exterior, inside its panelled walls inhaled school dinners,
the distinctive odour of years of sludge and slop.
Five hundred blue-beret'd, pre and apres pubescents
descended the stern gates to the ivy-clad grammar.
Lara, hopping off the 161 from Woolwich, only child

of discernible colour, did not notice her difference,
camouflaged by her uniform and the nattering swarm
of pink-flushed, off-white, horny girlies.

'Wish I had hair like yours, Soos. It's so nice.'
'Yeh, it's long but it goes haywire at night, La.
I used to scream like hell in the mornings. Truly!'
Theatrically, Susie tossed back her yellow mane,
brushed it effortlessly. 'Mum says it's my crowning glory.'
She jumped off the desk in the empty classroom, bent
over, hair dropped like a waterfall, she back combed it.
What was it like to see your hair in front of you, Lara
wondered. All she could do with hers was part it down
the middle and stick in stupid pins so it stayed put.
She hated her hair, couldn't even fit the school beret
on, it just bounced off. As for the boater – forget it!
'Yours is so soft and bouncy, Lara' Susie patted her head.
'See, just like a sponge. Amazing!' A surf of anger surged
through Lara at her bush. If only Susie knew how hard
it was to comb through its trillion stubborn tangles.
'Course, I have to wash mine every day else it gets greasy.
Dad says blondes have more fun but it's such a drag. Truly!'
The mane was bunched up for split-end inspection,
released, flicked over her right shoulder, shaken out,
flicked over her left shoulder, shaken out, flicked again.
Susie peered intensely at Lara's hair, said solemnly,
'You do wash your hair, don't you, La.' She sighed at Lara's
affirmative nod. 'Good!' She ruffled her mane, tossed it back.
'What's up, Lara? C'mon it might never happen.'

*

'Where'you from, La?' Susie suddenly asked
one lunch break on the playing fields. 'Woolwich.'
'No, silly, where are you from, y'know originally?'
'If you really must know I was born in Eltham, actually.'
'My dad says you must be from Jamaica,' Susie insisted.
'I'm not Jamaican! I'm English!' 'Then why are you coloured?'
Lara's heart shuddered, she felt so humiliated, so angry.
'Look, my father's Nigerian, my mother's English, alright!'
'So you're half-caste!' Lara tore at the grass in silence.
'Where's Nigeria then, is it near Jamaica?' 'It's in Africa.'
'Where's Africa exactly?' 'How should I know, I don't
bloody well live there, do I!' 'Is your dad from the jungle?'
That was it! Lara sprang up, brushed grass off her skirt,
pulled up her socks, flung her satchel over her shoulder,
stormed off. Susie ran after her. 'What's the matter, Lara?'
'You're bloody rude, that's the matter!' Tears were edging
their way out, blurred, she strode on. 'Well he could be
from the jungle, couldn't he?' Susie looked perplexed,
Lara felt so stupid blubbing in public. 'Look, I didn't mean
to hurt you, honest. I'm really sorry. Anyway, as far as
I'm concerned you're nearly white, alright? And I adore
your hair, it's like a brillo pad. Truly!' Lara stopped,
smiled, sighed, said, 'Race you to the tuck shop.
Last one there buys a packet of salt and vinegar.'

Home. I searched but could not find myself,
not on the screen, billboards, books, magazines,
and first and last not in the mirror, my demon, my love
which faded my brownness into a Bardot likeness.

Seasons of youth stirred in my cooking pot, a spicy
mix of marinated cultures, congealed into cold, disparate
lumps, untended, festered. The grandfather in the hall
measured hours, days, months, resonant metronome,
resounding up to my eyrie where I dragged my brain,
a stubborn rhino, into The Odyssey, revolutions
industrial, agricultural, French, British Royal lines
learnt by rote. Pigeons nested, jabbered, copulated,
fluttered off; cocooned under angular sliding ceilings,
my temple of youth, posters of those to die for, escape
from the madding crowd of da Costas who crammed
the Best Room, four brothers deliberately polluting,
the air with relentless noisy farts; showtime telly, gas fire's
hiss, escape, past the lofty Front Room, unused, jumbled,
home to two lonely pianos, a three-legged rocking horse,
moonshone bay windows, up three flights to the roof
where in the silence of the sky I longed for an image,
a story, to speak me, describe me, birth me whole.
Living in my skin, I was, but which one?

salt

Alice Walker

Never Offer Your Heart to Someone Who Eats Hearts

Never offer your heart
to someone who eats hearts
who finds heartmeat
delicious
but not rare
who sucks the juices
drop by drop
and bloody-chinned
grins
like a God.

Never offer your heart
to a heart gravy lover.
Your stewed, overseasoned
heart consumed
he will sop up your grief
with bread
and send it shuttling
from side to side
in his mouth
like bubblegum.

If you find yourself
in love
with a person
who eats hearts
these things
you must do:

Freeze your heart
immediately.
Let him – next time
he examines your chest –
find your heart cold
flinty and unappetizing.

Refrain from kissing
lest he in revenge
dampen the spark
in your soul.

Now,
sail away to Africa
where holy women
await you
on the shore –
long having practiced the art
of replacing hearts
with God
and Song.

Experiment

To find a remedy for a heart broken for the last time.

Method

Hurt my back taking down the boxes you stored in my attic;

Carefully unpack and repack them;

Drive 15 miles to the house you share with the woman you left me
    for;

Help you carry them up the stairs of your new lovenest;

Go home, drink peppermint tea, eat chocolate hobnobs and wait
    for

Results

Your voice on my machine, screeching over:

Trousers – cream linen, black leather and purple suede,

all now crotchless.

A lifetime of photographs reconfigured by Domestos, with

A julienne of negatives.

A rosewood occasional table infected with woodworm,

which isn't as easy to get hold of as one might think.

A smashed cut-glass bowl; a present from your grandmother,

the one who died last year.

Observations

For once your epithets don't sting.

Selfish, maybe.

Twisted, perhaps.

Fucked up, self-centred, vindictive bitch.

      Hmmm, do you know, I think you might have a point.

Conclusion

Go to bed and sleep the sleep of the righteous,

and if on waking I feel a little

guilty;

go into therapy and process away my guilt.

Like you do.

Pat Parker

My Lady Ain't No Lady

my lady ain't no lady

she doesn't flow into a room –
she enters & her presence is felt.
she doesn't sit small –
she takes all her space.
she doesn't partake of meals –
she eats – replenishes herself.

my lady ain't no lady –

she has been known
    to speak in loud voice,
    to pick her nose,
    stumble on a sidewalk,
    swear at her cats,
    swear at me,
    scream obscenities at men,
    paint rooms,
    repair houses,
    tote garbage,
    play basketball,
    & numerous other
    un lady like things.

my lady is definitely no lady
which is fine with me,

cause i ain't no gentleman.

Karen McCarthy

Fridge Theme

we will produce music
he said
blow some pole
shot rocks
cook
drool
boil an egg
eat chocolate
in bed
play live TV
be drunk
incubate
dress up in black diamonds
smear honey over her
delicate lust petals
flood
ache for
lazy summer
days
two
cool
together

merman

the day I married a merman, I led him down to the sea. said: swim as far out as you want to. and I waited. caught him sleeping on city streets. I licked his shiny skin. tasted salt on my lips. he said: I can't be here. this is not for me. the universe is not about this. I'm finding it so hard to breathe. still, he loved me like a warrior loved me like a child loved me in petals falling. the day I married a merman I led him down to the sea. saying: swim as far out as you want to. and I waited. days I could drink the sea. make you see me. knowing what would destroy you, would come right back and destroy me. so I sit by the water, as the sea becomes black and then blue, then black and then bluer. watch for a fin. or a glint of silver skin in the distance. tears come. catch them on my tongue. it's alright it's all right.the salt is proof that this was here. that you were real. that this was mine. and love is the constant essence of the waves. love, the constant essence of the waves. the day I married a merman, I led him down to the sea. said: swim as far out as you want to. I'm here.

44

love in la-la land

i miss you, pretty baby
freestylin your rhyme into my ear
stopping yourself from falling in love with me
cuz,
well cuz
of a strange warp in time
my love waz promised elsewhere.

but where is where?
when right now and then
i love you.

poets need poets to love
when words come hard (do i dare write this out loud?)

soft lips care for my thighs inner
my silk nightie danced all by itself
unaware it would catch tears tonight
as i feel your distance
your honesty in admitting that
it all started with alice coltrane
and ended in a long haul plane to london

w/me carrying a bare writing pad
and the shadows of your kisses semi-fossilised
upon the skin right above my bellybotton

flyin through the air a couple of hundred miles per hour
thinkin about doin our babies hair with green banana leaves
that bring fragrance to afro-tendrils.

*one should note that no other can
see the fossilised kisses.

this is priviledged soul information

available only to those
who have memorised the bass-lines to
queen coltrane's 'Journey in Satchidananda'

and besides you,
that narrows it down to
a few bass-players
or soothsayers,
too bad
for them
i'm a poet-digger.

Laureen Mar

Domestic Furniture

Contrary to popular opinion, domestic furniture
is not a dining table that also washes windows.

1.
Two chairs align themselves
with the table.
At first they sit perfectly
opposite each other,
opposite themselves,
each chair a mirror.

The table pretends to arbitrate:
this is the known circumference.
But casual objects –
a vase of antheriums *his*
favorite flowers, a telephone
bill *her calls* –
obscure the surface.

One chair skids around the corner,
All right, I'll come over, she said.

2.

The couch is full of cat hairs
They prowl around the couch like cats.
The couch is a teeter-totter,
The house, a sand-box.

Sit down, relax, smoke a cigarette.
All the while she feels
The white cat hairs grazing her black sweater,
The black cat hairs nuzzling her white skirt.
    No, she said, I won't.

Heart (W)rap

i strap my heart
tightly
bind it strong

tough
was how i presented it to you

how you questioned me
on what was in this strange parcel

first tentatively
and then held it in your hands
and feeling the warmth
and faint beat
you guessed

and since
have tugged at the string
i so carefully bound
in protection

how you teased open
layer after layer
unravelled it all
until it lay open before you

how you were repulsed
when you saw
the pale blood drained flesh

i too drew back

hardly recognising the half healed mass
before us
disgusted by the scars
you did not ask
in what battle they were won

but fled

'the faint hearted'
i whispered to myself
'won't inherit'

and began again
to bind

Karen McCarthy

Timetable

It is like being back at school again.
I am struggling with percentages: ratios, fractions.
I do not want to be there. I consider my lesson already learned.
(And what good will it all do me in the real world anyway?)
This is detention.
I am struggling with percentages.
The formulae don't work.

I have a lover.

> *He lives in a long, narrow apartment*
> *that is white but not bright.*
> *His city has harder edges.*
> *The angles are more acute.*

He has what is first described as a situation.
My **ENGLISH** comprehension skills
are better than my
MATHS
I know now, that means wife.

(For God's sake, give me a
BREAK)

CHEMISTRY
There has been a physical separation.
Which is less than or equal to ours
Depending on your
GEOGRAPHY
But it exists without the litmus of paper.
(We schoolkids know nothing of the law.)

I am struggling with percentages.
Equations. Differentials.

> *There can be no equilateral triangle.*
> *The coordinates are awry.*

He is not 100 per cent sure about anything.
Least of all his situation.
HISTORY
takes its own time

(There is no such thing as a free
LUNCH)

> *Come on,*
> *we both know that*

Out there on the playing fields things aren't much better.

GAMES

It's *always* cold on a hockey pitch.
Survival of the fittest.
I have conducted empirical statistical research you see.
And empirically speaking the data is
   incontrovertible.
This is not multiple choice. Shit.
A, B, C or D gives me a 25 per cent chance of being right
even if I've done no fucking homework for the past three years.

But the galling thing is that this time I have.
A mature student.
It doesn't do to bunk off. ('The only loser would be me.')
I have been uncharacteristically diligent.
No need to

      try harder

I do not disrupt the class any more.
I do not answer back.
I will not answer back.

     (repeat x 500)

I am battling with percentages:
variables, probabilities.
The problem is
this is an examination
and I am running out of time.

Patience Agbabi

Sentences

'I now pronounce you Man and Wife'
said the vicar 'You may kiss the bride'
and he raises her veil of gossamer white
and he kisses her lips
for he is a Man and she is a Wife
so for him to kiss her it is his right
and everyone smiles and the ring shines bright
on the finger where he placed it
and the family album reveals the white
teeth of the smile of the happily married couple
not her womanhood buried out of sight

So now their love is legitimate legal
in the eyes of society unequal

They begin to live their married life
they both go to work cos they have to survive
he spends his money on having fun outside
she spends hers on the home cos she is the wife
but the wedding presents make it alright
a microwave oven a blender
and an excellent chopping knife

A syncopated heart beat
she's expecting a baby their love is complete

And he comes home pissed from the pub one night
and she asks him why he's late
and he hates to be questioned about his life
he slaps her a bit to keep her quiet
she doesn't really put up a fight
then he puts it in her and pushes with all his might
and she closes her eyes and lips so tight
and when he's finished he turns off the light
covering up his huge love bite

And now their love is beginning to die
she loses the child and nobody questions why

And the years go by and she has to survive
though she often thinks of taking her life
she called the police round the other night
they took him in but they sympathised with him
then he says he's sorry and she thinks it's alright
and they say that his bark is worse than his bite
but she thinks of the bruises she has to hide
and she knows that that wedding camera lied
when it showed her smiling fat and wide

And now their love has completely gone
but worse and worse the marriage goes on

And he comes home pissed from the pub one night
and she's gone to bed and turned off the light
and he turns it on again out of spite
and says 'Open your legs you bitch it's my right
cos I'm a man and you're my wife'
so she punches him in the face with all her might
and leaves a bruise
but he holds her round the neck too tight
to be an embrace and he says
'If you do that again I'll fucking kill you alright'

And now their love has changed to hate
and it seems like another age and time
that they went on that first shy date

And her mother says 'He ought to be locked up inside'
and her father 'He should pick on someone his own size'
and her brother doesn't know what he's like
and her sister says 'Divorce him'
and she knows her sister's right
but she's scared what her man would do
and in spite of it all
she has her pride

And he comes home pissed from the pub one night
and he doesn't even speak
just beats her with his fists
and when she asks him why he has to fight
he says 'You're married to me for life'

then she knows that he knows that she spoke
to her solicitor on the phone the other night
And she cannot believe that this is her married life
he sees the hatred in her eyes
and he laughs and falls
and the last glimmer of hope inside her dies

She goes to the kitchen
and sees in the microwave oven
his dried up dinner
sees the broken blender
and the excellent chopping knife

The ring shines bright on the finger
where he placed it
but she holds the knife in her right
and when she stabs him
she stabs him with all her might
and anger

'I now pronounce you Man and Wife'
sentenced the vicar
the judge said 'Life'
and she turned in her grave
cos she knew she'd been sentenced
twice

Jackie Kay

Other Lovers

1 *What was it you said again there by the river*

And later, when the young danced to an old song,
the moon split in two, the stars smashed,
what was it again?

By the river, by the procession of trees,
the shadow marching across your face,
how deep do you feel?

I hold the light hetween us. Kiss you
hard in the dark. Ahead of us the bright blue eyes of sheep.
Are there words for this? Words that sink to the bottom

of the river where ducks flap their sudden wings,
startle silence; believe me, believe me.
We walk this night, shining our bright eye ahead.
Do you love me, love me, do you.

2 *The Day You Change*

The lace curtains go up.
She starts saying *you always say;*

you realise you always do.
On the living wall, strange shapes spread
like those on hospital sheets.

She closes the curtain round herself;
you hold your hand against the side or your cheek.
Tonight, you eat an instant meal
(no long spaghetti, no candles.)
Conversation limited

to *pass the pepper*. In the bedroom
the cover is stretched taut,
pulled back and forth in a battle,
till the small hours leaves one of you cold.
How long is a night like this?

3 *When you move out*

You mark each box with a thick black pen.
You will always be neat, no matter what's said.
And fair. You do not pack what is not yours.
Even the joint presents: the Chinese vase,
the white dinner plates, the samovar,
you leave to her. You won't miss things.

At night you will lie on a different side.
Listen to another station to send you to sleep.
You will never play Nina Simone, again.

Other things won't be possible. Restaurants,
parks, cinemas, pubs. Avoid them. They are dangerous.
Never go near another garden. There's no point,

growing peonies to blossom without you. Delphiniums.
Take up something else. *It doesn't matter what.*

4 *Swim*

So, at the end of a perfect rainbow
you have upped and left, and I
have taken to swimming a hundred
lengths of breast-stroke per day.
This is the way of love.
Even swimming, I am obsessed
with the way your feet are
when stroked, your legs,
the long length of them,
how I could have you all worked
up in seconds. My fingers
doing the butterfly, you saying,
Don't stop Don't stop Don't stop.

5 *She never thought she could with anyone else*

And now, here she is, whispering urgently into another ear.
Holding someone else tight. After the sixth month,
she returns the *I love you*, she's heard since day one.

In your island she lies in the sun like a traitor.
But you are always standing on her shoulders.
She starts to do things the way you did them.
She stacks dishes in order of size.
She begins to like your favourite cheese.
In restaurants she chooses the wine you chose.
She finds herself getting irritated
at the way her new lover makes a bed.
She misses smooth corners, no creases.
She scrubs the bath twice a day, and at night,
sees the wrong lover mouthing her name.

6 *Worse than that*

One day you find you are your other lover.
You use exactly ther same expressions,
like a child uses its mother's.
You disapprove of the same things. Refuse
to laugh at certain jokes. Uncertain
of yourself now, you start to imitate an absence.
You don't know what to think of the News.
Your world lacks gravity. Her presence.
You drop yourself from a height. Don't fall.
You are scared to go from A to B
– she was the map-reader.
You're scared of new things to eat.
You poke at them on your plate, depressed.
Long for your favourite meal, a simple life;

until you learn to cook on your own
and it's good (though you say it yourself)
Out and about you are so confident
you're taking short cuts, back alleys,
winding your way past yourself,
up a narrow cobbled close into the big High Street.
You stand, looking down, the air bursting
through your raincoat like a big balloon.
You manage to fathom one of those machines. *Easy.*
Catch your slick tenners, *No bother,*
and saunter off, whistling to yourself.

You have actually done it.
You would never have believed it.
You have a whole new life.

earth

Patience Agbabi

Ufo Woman
(pronounced oofoe)

First World meets Third World
Third World meets First World

Mother Earth. Heath Row. Terminal 5. Yo!
Do I look hip in my space-hopper-green
slingbacks, iridescent sky-blue-pink skin
pants and hologram hair cut? Can I have
my clothes back when you've finished with them, please?
Hello! I just got offa the space ship.

I've learnt the language, read the VDU
and watched the video twice. Mother Earth
do *you* read *me?* Why then stamp my passport
ALIEN at Heath Row? Did I come third
in the World Race? Does my iridescent
sky-blue-pink skin embarrass you, mother?

LONDON. Meandering the streets paved with
hopscotch and butterscotch, kids with crystal
cut ice-cream cones and tin can eyes ask 'Why
don't U F O back to your own planet?'
Streets paved with NF (no fun) grafitti
Nefertiti go home from the old days.

So I take a tram, tube, train, taxi trip
hip-hugged, bell-bottomed and thick-lipped, landing
in a crazy crazy cow pat. SUSSEX.
Possibly it's my day-glo afro, rich
as a child paints a tree in full foliage
that makes them stare with flying saucer eyes.

Perhaps my antennae plaits in Winter
naked twigs cocooned in thread for bigger
better hair makes them dare to ask to touch.
'*Can we touch your hair?*' Or not ask at all;
my two-tone hand with its translucent palm,
lifeline, heartline, headline, children, journeys,

prompting the '*Why's it white on the inside
of your hand? Do you wash? Does it wash off?*'
Or my core names. Trochaic, Dactylic,
Galactic beats from ancient poetry,
names they make me repeat, make them call me
those sticks-and-stones-may-break-my-bones-but names.

In times of need I ask the oracle.
Withdrawing to my work station I press
HELP. I have just two options. HISTORY:
The screen flashes subliminal visuals
from the old days which I quickly translate:
Slave ship:space ship, racism:spacism.

Resignedly I select HERSTORY:
the screen displays a symmetrical tree
which has identical roots and branches.
I can no longer reason, only feel
not aloneness but oneness. I decide
to physically process this data.

So I take the train plane to the Equator
the Motherland, travel 5 degrees North
to the GO SLOW quick-talking fast-living
finger-licking city known as LAGOS.
Streets paved with gold-threaded gold-extensioned
women and silk-suited men; market-stalls

of red, orange, yellow and indigo.
Perhaps it's not my bold wild skin colour,
well camouflaged in this spectrum of life,
but the way I wear my skin, too uptight,
too did-I-wear-the-right-outfit-today?
too I-just-got-off-the-last-London-flight;

or my shy intergalactic lingo
my monospeak, my verbal vertigo
that makes them stare with flying saucer eyes.
They call me Ufo woman, oyinbo
from the old days which translates as weirdo,
white, outsider, other, and I withdraw

into myself, no psychedelic shield,
no chameleonic facade, just raw.
Then I process Ufo and U F O,
realise the former is a blessing:
the latter a curse. I rename myself
Ufo Woman and touch base at Heath Row.

No. Don't bother to strip, drug, bomb search me
I'm not staying this time. Why press rewind?
Why wait for First World homo sapiens
to cease their retroactive spacism?
Their world may be a place worth fighting for
I suggest in the next millennium.

So, smart casual, I prepare for lift off,
in my fibre optic firefly Levis,
my sci-fi hi-fi playing *Revelations*
and my intergalactic mobile ON.
Call me. I'll be surfing the galaxy
searching for that perfect destination.

Excerpt from Elmina Castle: Cape Coast, Ghana

n a warm breeze
de of clay.
t trails and candleflies
om the neonlights

'ast? Tense.
ne shifted like a continent.
d the unfathomable
a lassoed notion
f the sacred cow,
ng in virgin hay
ortable with the burn of the rope
the noose.

ckwards through the temple of my head
flight will leave me gaping.
een my brows is birthed out my mouth
moans and uttering wind chimes
    when to hush   as the pain leaves.
ng the blues already knows.
ird place to call home.

lfather suffering with high pressure and

t and watches Carnival on TV
in but never changing the channel,
hey're dancing like Africans,
e for the bedroom'.
s

arthritic hands,

Gotta make a way out of no way –
traditional black folk saying

The Journey

There is no perfect
past to go back to. Each time I look
into your eyes, I see the long hesitation
of ten thousand years, our mothers' mothers
sitting under the shade trees on boxes, waiting.
There is some great question in your eye that no
longer needs asking: the ball
glistening, wet; the black iris
intense. We know the same things.
What you wait for, I wait for

The Tour
The castle, always on an
outcrop of indifference;

human shells,
the discards on the way.

Where our mothers were held, we walk now
as tourists, looking for cokes, film, the bathroom.

A few steps beyond the brutalization, we
stand in the sun:

   This area for tourists only.

Our very presence an ironic
point of interest to our guide.

Tourists' Lunch
On a rise, overlooking
the past, we eat
jolaf with pepper sauce and chicken,
laugh, drink beer, fold our dresses
up under us and bathe thigh-
deep in the weary Atlantic.

Post-Carib

I've become one of those transp
that withers in English cold.
Newly unaccustomed to a lifetir
where the sky knows more shad
rain is never warm and trees ar
A New World black soul
that can't recall the reasons for
Just give me soft water to bathe
coconut water to drink in,
sea water to pray in.
I want to see sun resting on fert
while I'm swinging my skirts
to tempos of drum and steel.
I want to pull green oranges, cu
and mangoes from the trees
with cousin Jerry who has more
After the market we eat rice and
in a two room house filled with
Tell me again Tante, tell me aga
of herbs, roots and history.
Tell me again.

I disappeared
with a man m
Blue moonlig
led me away f
I used to love
Yes, used to.
Something in
I started to fe
slowly pulling
into the barn
together nestl
till it was com
and absolving

A crow flies b
and I fear the
The knot betw
in a chorus of
that know not
Here's someth
I've found a t

My father's go
 redundanc
sits on his hea
Feigning disd
complaining
those moves a
His wife finge
her rosary wit

snaps commands
at the kitchen help they can't
afford.
Bandits and God have the masses living in fear.
Mismanaged resources have made all that ain't free too dear.
So while I lime on the promenade in a state of bacchanal grace,
survivors rummage through rubbish, hovering vulturine
    for my waste.
Carib returned, 20 cents a bottle. . .
'Psssst Reds,
God'll bless you on the other side.
On the other side Reds.
God bless you.
Bless you Reds.'

Rosamond S King

Eating Dahl Poori Roti

heat it
in the microwave
(freeze 'ethnic food' rations
so they last)
bend towards the heat
approach the skin folded
around potato
as if it were a lover's nipple.

What else can be delected
folded daintily whole
torn apart and thrust in finger
fulls or tasted w/ a knife and fork?

I tell my mother eating
the food of my people
makes me so happy it is
better than sex. She asks me
How would you know?

Jackie Kay

In my country

walking by the waters
down where an honest river
shakes hands with the sea,
a woman passed round me
in a slow watchful circle,
as if I were a superstition;

or the worst dregs of her imagination,
so when she finally spoke
her words spliced into bars
of an old wheel. A segment of air.
Where do you come from?
'Here,' I said, 'Here. These parts.'

Land to Light On

Vi

Maybe this wide country just stretches your life to a thinness
just trying to take it in, trying to calculate in it what you must
do, the airy bay at its head scatters your thoughts like someone
going mad from science and birds pulling your hair, ice invades
your nostrils in chunks, land fills your throat, you are so busy
with collecting the north, scrambling to the Arctic so wilfully, so
busy getting a handle to steady you to this place you get blown
into bays and lakes and and fissures you have yet to see, except
on a map in a schoolroom long ago but you have a sense that
whole parts of you are floating in heavy lake water heading for
what you suspect is some other life that lives there, and you, you
only trust moving water and water that reveals itself in colour.
It always takes long to come to what you have to say, you have to
sweep this stretch of land up around your feet and point to the
signs, pleat whole histories with pins in your mouth and guess
at the fall of words.

Vii

But the sight of land has always baffled you,
there is dirt somewhere older than any exile
and try as you might, your eyes only compose

Toi Derricote

Excerpt from Elmina Castle: Cape Coast, Ghana

Gotta make a way out of no way —
traditional black folk saying

The Journey

There is no perfect
past to go back to. Each time I look
into your eyes, I see the long hesitation
of ten thousand years, our mothers' mothers
sitting under the shade trees on boxes, waiting.
There is some great question in your eye that no
longer needs asking: the ball
glistening, wet; the black iris
intense. We know the same things.
What you wait for, I wait for

The Tour
The castle, always on an
outcrop of indifference;

human shells,
the discards on the way.

Where our mothers were held, we walk now
as tourists, looking for cokes, film, the bathroom.

A few steps beyond the brutalization, we
stand in the sun:

> *This area for tourists only.*

Our very presence an ironic
point of interest to our guide.

Tourists' Lunch
On a rise, overlooking
the past, we eat
jolaf with pepper sauce and chicken,
laugh, drink beer, fold our dresses
up under us and bathe thigh-
deep in the weary Atlantic.

Vanessa Richards

Post-Caribbean Reds

I've become one of those transplanted tropical flowers
that withers in English cold.
Newly unaccustomed to a lifetime spent above the 54th parallel
where the sky knows more shades of grey than blue,
rain is never warm and trees are evergreen.
A New World black soul
that can't recall the reasons for a big city career.
Just give me soft water to bathe in,
coconut water to drink in,
sea water to pray in.
I want to see sun resting on fertile hills
while I'm swinging my skirts
to tempos of drum and steel.
I want to pull green oranges, custard apples
and mangoes trom the trees
with cousin Jerry who has more fingers than teeth.
After the market we eat rice and beans
in a two room house filled with family, laughter and kerosene.
Tell me again Tante, tell me again
of herbs, roots and history.
Tell me again.

I disappeared in a warm breeze
with a man made of clay.
Blue moonlight trails and candleflies
led me away from the neonlights
I used to love
Yes, used to. Past? Tense.
Something in me shifted like a continent.
I started to feel the unfathomable
slowly pulling a lassoed notion
into the barn of the sacred cow,
together nestling in virgin hay
till it was comfortable with the burn of the rope
and absolving the noose.

A crow flies backwards through the temple of my head
and I fear the flight will leave me gaping.
The knot between my brows is birthed out my mouth
in a chorus of moans and uttering wind chimes
that know not   when to hush   as the pain leaves.
Here's something the blues already knows.
I've found a third place to call home.

My father's godfather suffering with high pressure and
    redundancy
sits on his heart and watches Carnival on TV
Feigning disdain but never changing the channel,
complaining 'they're dancing like Africans,
those moves are for the bedroom'.
His wife fingers
her rosary with arthritic hands,

snaps commands
at the kitchen help they can't
afford.
Bandits and God have the masses living in fear.
Mismanaged resources have made all that ain't free too dear.
So while I lime on the promenade in a state of bacchanal grace,
survivors rummage through rubbish, hovering vulturine
   for my waste.
Carib returned, 20 cents a bottle...
'Psssst   Reds,
God'll bless you on the other side.
On the other side Reds.
God bless you.
Bless you Reds.'

Rosamond S King

Eating Dahl Poori Roti

heat it
in the microwave
(freeze 'ethnic food' rations
so they last)
bend towards the heat
approach the skin folded
around potato
as if it were a lover's nipple.

What else can be delected
folded daintily whole
torn apart and thrust in finger
fulls or tasted w/ a knife and fork?

I tell my mother eating
the food of my people
makes me so happy it is
better than sex. She asks me
How would you know?

Jackie Kay

In my country

walking by the waters
down where an honest river
shakes hands with the sea,
a woman passed round me
in a slow watchful circle,
as if I were a superstition;

or the worst dregs of her imagination,
so when she finally spoke
her words spliced into bars
of an old wheel. A segment of air.
Where do you come from?
'Here,' I said, 'Here. These parts.'

Land to Light On

Vi

Maybe this wide country just stretches your life to a thinness
just trying to take it in, trying to calculate in it what you must
do, the airy bay at its head scatters your thoughts like someone
going mad from science and birds pulling your hair, ice invades
your nostrils in chunks, land fills your throat, you are so busy
with collecting the north, scrambling to the Arctic so wilfully, so
busy getting a handle to steady you to this place you get blown
into bays and lakes and and fissures you have yet to see, except
on a map in a schoolroom long ago but you have a sense that
whole parts of you are floating in heavy lake water heading for
what you suspect is some other life that lives there, and you, you
only trust moving water and water that reveals itself in colour.
It always takes long to come to what you have to say, you have to
sweep this stretch of land up around your feet and point to the
signs, pleat whole histories with pins in your mouth and guess
at the fall of words.

Vii

But the sight of land has always baffled you,
there is dirt somewhere older than any exile
and try as you might, your eyes only compose

the muddy drain in front of the humid almond
tree, the unsettling concrete sprawl of the housing
scheme, the stone your uncle used to smash his name
into another uncle's face, your planet is your hands
your house behind your eyebrows and the tracing
paper over the bead of islands of indifferent and
reversible shapes, now Guadeloupe is a crab pinched
at the waist, now Nevis' borders change by mistake
and the carelessness of history, now sitting in Standard
Five, the paper shifting papery in the sweat of your
fingers you come to be convinced that these lines will
not matter, your land is a forced march on the bottom
of the Sargasso, your way tangled in life

V iii
I am giving up on land to light on, it's only true, it is only
something someone tells you, someone you should not trust
anyway. Days away, years before, a beer at your lips and the view
from Castara, the ocean as always pulling you towards its bone
and much later, in between, learning to drive the long drive
to Burnt River, where the land is not beautiful, braised
like the back of an animal, burnt in coolness, but the sky is,
like the ocean pulling you toward its bone, skin falling away
from your eyes, you see it without its history of harm, without
its damage, or everywhere you walk on the earth there's harm,
everywhere resounds. This is the only way you will know
the names of cities, not charmed or overwhelmed, all you see is
museums of harm and metros full, in Paris, walls inspected
crudely for dates, and Amsterdam, street corners full of

druggists, ashen with it, all the way from Suriname, Curaçao,
Dutch and German inking their lips, pen nibs of harm blued in
the mouth, not to say London's squares, blackened in statues,
Zeebrugge, searching the belly of fish, Kinshasa, through an
airplane window the dictator cutting up bodies grips the plane
to the tarmac and I can't get out to kiss the ground.

Viv
This those slaves must have known who were my mothers, skin
falling from their eyes, they moving toward their own bone,
"so thank god for the ocean and the sky all implicated, all
unconcerned," they must have said, "or there'd be nothing to
love." How they spent a whole lifetime undoing the knot
of a word and as fast it would twirl up again, spent
whole minutes inching their eyes above sea level only
for latitude to shift, only for a horrible horizon to list, thank god
for the degrees of the chin, the fooling plane of doorway, only
the mind, the not just simple business of return and turning,
that is for scholars and indecisive frigates, circling and circling,
stripped in their life, naked as seaweed, they would have sat
and sunk but no, the sky was a doorway, a famine and a jacket,
the sea a definite post

V v
I'm giving up on the land to light on, slowly, it isn't land,
it is the same as fog and mist and figures and lines
and erasable thoughts, it is buildings and governments
and toilets and front door mats and typewriter shops,
cards with your name and clothing that comes undone,

skin that doesn't fasten and spills and shoes. It's paper,
paper, maps. Maps that get wet and rinse out, in my hand
anyway. I'm giving up what was always shifting, mutable
cities' fluorescences, limbs, chalk curdled blackboards
and carbon copies, wretching water, cunning walls. Books
to set it right. Look. What I know is this. I'm giving up.
No offence. I was never committed. Not ever, to offices
or islands, continents, graphs, whole cloth, these sequences
or even footsteps.

V vi
Light passes through me lightless, sound soundless,
smoking nowhere, groaning with sudden birds. Paper
dies, flesh melts, leaving stockings and their useless vanity
in graves, bodies lie still across foolish borders.
I'm going my way, going my way gleaning shade, burnt
meridians, dropping carets, flung latitudes, inattention,
screeching looks. I'm trying to put my tongue on dawns
now, I'm busy licking dusk away, tracking deep twittering
silences. You come to this, here's the marrow of it, not
moving, not standing, it's too much to hold up, what I
really want to say is, I don't want no fucking country, here
or there and all the way back, I don't like it, none of it,
easy as that. I'm giving up on land to light on, and why not,
I can't perfect my own shadow, my violent sorrow, my
individual wrists.

Parm Kaur

Lines of Origin

Before I could see
I could feel

    thick jagged lines.

Before I could speak
I could see

    jagged, red purple lines.

Before I could walk
I swam in a sea of

    jagged, red purple lines.

Outside I wore a
translucent cloak of

    jagged red purple lines.

It tripped me up, it
weighed me down, this cloak of

    jagged red purple lines.

Often lost in dark caves
led by haunting whispers,
I wandered finally
burning from my eyes a
veil of red purple lines

and saw.
    They were the lines

of my mother, her mother,
her mother's mother and
so all mothers of each
corner of the globe
in this translucent cloak
of

    jagged red purple lines.

Then I put down the cloak
of

    jagged red purple

scars and learnt to walk

    lightly.

Amiti Grech

Two Gardens

My spirit still warm
from my body's presence
in a garden
where parakeets pecked
sunflower seeds,
and dusk dilated
tuberose scent,
recollection vivid
as this moment
in an English garden
where roses
seal summer
to the fullest,
tropic zone and temperate meet.

forest

Rita Dove

The Bistro Styx

She was thinner, with a mannered gauntness
as she paused just inside the double
glass doors to survey the room, silvery cape
billowing dramatically behind her. *What's this,*

I thought, lifting a hand until
she nodded and started across the parquet;
that's when I saw she was dressed all in gray,
from a kittenish cashmere skirt and cowl

down to the graphite signature of her shoes.
'Sorry I'm late,' she panted, though
she wasn't, sliding into the chair, her cape

tossed off in a shudder of brushed steel.
We kissed. Then I leaned back to peruse
my blighted child, this wary aristocratic mole.

'How's business?' I asked, and hazarded
 a motherly smile to keep from crying out:
Are you content to conduct your life
as a cliché and, what's worse,

an anachronism, the brooding artist's demimonde?
Near the rue Princesse they had opened
a gallery *cum* souvenir shop which featured
fuzzy off-color Monets next to his acrylics, no doubt,

plus bearded African drums and the occasional miniature
gargoyle from Notre Dame the Great Artist had
carved at breakfast with a pocket knife.

'Tourists love us. The Parisians, of course' –
she blushed – 'are amused, though not without
a certain admiration…'

                              The Chateaubriand

arrived on a bone-white plate, smug and absolute
in its fragrant crust, a black plug steaming
like the heart plucked from the chest of a worthy enemy;
one touch with her fork sent pink juices streaming.

'Admiration for what?' Wine, a bloody
Pinot Noir, brought color to her cheeks. 'Why,
the aplomb with which we've managed
to support our Art' – meaning he'd convinced

her to pose nude for his appalling canvases,
faintly futuristic landscapes strewn
with carwrecks and bodies being chewed

by rabid cocker spaniels. 'I'd like to come by
the studio,' I ventured, 'and see the new stuff.'
'Yes, if you wish…' A delicate rebuff

before the warning: 'He dresses all
in black now. Me, he drapes in blues and carmine –
and even though I think it's kinda cute,
in company I tend toward more muted shades.'

She paused and had the grace
to drop her eyes. She did look ravishing,
spookily insubstantial, a lipstick ghost on tissue,
or as if one stood on a fifth-floor terrace

peering through a fringe of rain at Paris'
dreaming chimney pots, each sooty issue
wobbling skyward in an ecstatic oracular spiral.

'And he never thinks of food. I wish
I didn't have to plead with him to eat…' Fruit
and cheese appeared, arrayed on leaf-green dishes.

I stuck with café crème. 'This Camembert's
so ripe,' she joked, 'it's practically grown hair,'
mucking a golden glob complete with parsley sprig
onto a heel of bread. Nothing seemed to fill

her up: She swallowed, sliced into a pear,
speared each tear-shaped lavaliere
and popped the dripping mess into her pretty mouth.
Nowhere the bright tufted fields, weighted

vines and sun poured down out of the south.
'But are you happy?' Fearing I whispered it
quickly. 'What? You know, Mother' –

she bit into the starry rose of a fig –
'one really should try the fruit here.'
I've lost her, I thought, and called for the bill.

Melvina Hazard

Unnamed

1.
i remember she.
sitting on the old basket chair
or maybe it was a hammock...
the poison burning away at her insides
while she sat there
smoking a broadway

ma.
that was what i called she
as a child she was unnamed by the anglicans
just as her mother was unnamed by
the fat sweaty indian agent at the dockside

she voice.
like red gravel scraping
the cracked barber greene
pelting rebukes at the dozens
of grandchildren whose names she
could never remember
because she was listening to the
voices of her dead parents
who called her beti
but whose names she never knew

I remember she
my grandmother
sitting on the old basket chair
or maybe it was a hammock
but that is all i remember of her
that and skipping over the
soft dirt of her grave when i was four
and on her tombstone
the name that was never hers to begin with
but which she is remembered by
i never knew her name

2.
i am aften mispronounced
in common conversation
what is your name they ask
then turn
to continue
a sentence with a stranger
who just happens
to be passing by

my name is often misspelt
in legal documents
lazy public servants can't be bothered
by repetition
they turn away
and write
my unname
on a blank piece of paper

my name is my name is my name is
i forget

S Lee Yung

Vignettes

She'd say
'Always eat in
    SILENCE'
Ne'er do or say violent
    things on Chinese
    celebrations
Even though I felt
    like yelling NO!
'Stay home and cook the meals,
    do the house chores
& you'll marry someday.'

Daddy was Americanized
    who fought in WWII
    North Africa
    lik'd gamblin'
    drivin' to the countryside
    'n go fishin'.
He'd live in the attic
    with *House & Garden*
    next to his bed,
    wanting to forget the so-called

responsibility of three children
Just gettin' drunk
      & ramblin' on & on
          to defy racism.

Only,
once on Xmas, makin' a night visit
I heard Daddy
whistled and tiptoed
    into the house
He set two velvet boxes
    on the desk
& I stood up on my crib
'Daddy, teach me to whistle'
He told me to
    'Curl your tongue
    tighten your lips
    & whistle.'
He left behind
    one cameo set
    the gold wrapped
    round the black stone,
    the other inset with a
    faceted pink glass
    in a fleur-de-lis shell,
    sparklin' the eye
His daughters felt like ladies
    of exquisite design
    but never have you heard
    my whistled melody.

They argued
    while watchin'
'Father Knows Best'
My eyes glued to the screen
My ears filled with their
    shouts, their
    decision pulling the
    family   apart
    screamin' of who
    knows best
My tongue knotted
Just holding back
    as I saw a mother
    a father hug each
    other, turn &
    smile at their
    bubbly children &
then wave to the audience

She left the Northwest coastline,
    once matched, married &
    divorced
She took her children
    to New York
    & she learned to
    throw sadness away
    she remarried.

We never mentioned the sorrow of
    leaving home
    because we always
    ate in
    SILENCE.

Karen McCarthy

Passport

You are not indelible. I saw the photograph:
your pre-independence passport – (1957) – when you passed port.
Your face – out of place. Looking freer then.
Tick-tock. Bee-bop. Discord. A-chord. Recall.
                                The un-rub-out-able record.
Remember. Dismember. Take apart. Can't get to the heart.

Remember. Dismember. Take apart. Have to get to the heart
of this remarkable transfiguration. I find the mark.
                                Can't see the mark-ee.
5–5,6–6, 7,8, 9. Quick time.
Numbers numb me. Hide the memory.
I see you before you saw me (Tick-tock, take-stock).

I saw you before you see me (Take stock, tick-tock).
Can I recognize the slick zoot suit?
Looking fine, see your skin shine.
Yeah, looks like you knew how to have a good time.
And then. Forty years.

Forty years. And then.
Multiple patriarch. Mr Mack. Daddy.
You are no Johnny come lately.
Johnny gone long time.
I never saw him before. But you know who he is.

Olive Senior

Hurricane Story, 1988

My mother wasn't christened
Imelda but she stashed a cache
of shoes beneath the bed.

She used to travel to Haiti,
Panama, Curacao, Miami,
wherever there was bargain

to catch – even shoes that
didn't have match. Back home
she could always find customer

come bend-down to look and talk
where she plant herself on
sidewalk. When the hurricane

hit, she ban her belly and bawl,
for five flights a day to Miami
grounded. No sale and her shoes

getting junjo from the damp (since
the roof decamp) and the rest
sitting in Customs, impounded.

My mother banked between her
breasts, lived out her dreams
in a spliff or two each night.

Since the storm, things so tight
her breasts shrivel, the notes
shrinking. Every night she there

thinking. Every morning she get up
and she wail: Lawd! Life so soak-up
and no bail out. To raatid!

Grace Nichols

Why Shouldn't She?

My mother loved cooking
but hated washing up
Why shouldn't she?
  cooking was an art
she could move her lips to
then the pleasure
feeding the proverbial
multitude (us)
on less than a loaf
and two fishes

Jackie Kay

Keeping Orchids

The orchids my mother gave me when we first met
are still alive, twelve days later. Although

some of the buds remain closed as secrets.
Twice since I carried them back, like a baby in a shawl,

from her train station to mine, then home. Twice
since then the whole glass carafe has crashed

falling over, unprovoked, soaking my chest of drawers.
All the broken waters. I have rearranged

the upset orchids with troubled hands. Even after
that the closed ones did not open out. The skin

shut like an eye in the dark; the closed lid.
Twelve days later, my mother's hands are all I have.

Her face is fading fast. Even her voice rushes
through a tunnel the other way from home.

I close my eyes and try to remember exactly:
a paisley pattern scarf, a brooch, a navy coat.

A digital watch her daughter was wearing when she died.
Now they hang their heads,

and suddenly grow old   the proof of meeting. Still,
her hands, awkward and hard to hold

fold and unfold a green carrier bag as she tells
the story of her life. Compressed. Airtight.

A sad square, then a crumpled shape. A bag of tricks.
Her secret life – a hidden album, a box of love letters.

A door opens and closes. Time is outside waiting.
I catch the draught in my winter room.

Airlocks keep the cold air out.
Boiling water makes flowers live longer. So does

cutting the stems with a sharp knife.

Janet Kofi-Tsekpo

Father

Man Friday
works harder than my sex.

Who are you?
Silent and agile, your

name kept like
a sharp tool. I use it

as a play-
thing. When I call you come

stumbling in-
to my mind, and I stuff

words in your
mouth like pregnant pillows.

I really want to de-
construct you,

pull your plump thoughts apart
and push through

those taut muscles to your
felt flesh. Do

you hear? The ocean rocks
around your

feet; it roars and sighs. I
fill your ab-

sences with harsh tongues. Who
belongs to

whom – fumbling
over a restless dream,

as horses
crash on the wet black shore –

who rules now
on this island of night?

electricity

Rita Dove

Particulars

She discovered she felt better
if the simplest motions
had their origin in agenda –
second coffee at nine or eating just
the top half of the muffin, no butter
with blueberry jam. She caught herself
crying every morning, ten sharp, as if
the weather front had swerved,
a titanic low pressure system
moving in as night steamed off
and left a day wih nothing else
to fill it but moisture. She wept
steadily, and once
she recognized the pattern,
took care to be in one spot waiting
a few moments before. They weren't
tears of relief, and after a few weeks
not even of a particular sorrow.
*We never learn a secret until
it's useless*, she thought, and perhaps
that was what she was weeping over:
the lack of conclusion,
the eternal *dénouement*.

Melvina Hazard

Mal Yeux

(Performance Piece)

So what!
If yuh say I'se a sadist
If I have blue ink stained hater blood inside meh
Yuh tink yuh could fuck meh-mock meh-poyah meh –
Slash yuh heavy blue-black bad bwoy fists
All over meh body
LALUNECOWRE JOUVRAWAY
Yeah, come J'ouvert mornin'
Yuh better line-up-wine-up-stand-up-for a quickie
Ent is man yuh name man?
But first yuh'll have to genuflect before the bluest of the blue
Goddess Kali disguised as the Virgin Mary before
She drown yuh in the black mud between
The jab jab devil and the deep blue Caribbean Sea.

Blue Blue I love you.

Mal Yeux is me, Ms Mal Yeux to you.
Yuh could evil-eye meh
Hang out dem totem telephone radar poles to try and control me
Try to electrically conduct yuh weak white light combustile
    chemistry
through my eagerly awaiting, lustfully heaving body

Even adorn me with a numeric identity
But when I unleash my ice-blue vex rage disguised as an army of
Pretty jabmolassies on a neo-nazi feminist rampage –
Yuh go see!

Listen dred, I ent no fuckin' Weepin' Willow or shuddering Tia
    Marie
Better watch yuh back, jack, an call meh Stinkin' Susie
I'll never Jump-and-Kiss-you –
I'll sooner Rose thorn rip out yuh heart
Rather than raise the white flag to you
I vex til I blue – I blue, blue, blue vex
When I see you through my jaundiced third eye Kali vision
I see school boy semen stained blonde bimbos
In a *Playboy* magazine and your
Fucked-up racist, supremacist crap
Crumpled up like tissue paper between the sheets
Born to be porn – born to be blue-balled

Better get out the Phillips Milk of Magnesia bottle and
Stick it up yuh AHHHHHH...

– Piece of burnt out dried bamboo out in the kitchen garden
Cause if I see you before you see me,
Den is ded yuh ded, dred, cause when yuh beat a woman
'Til every inch of she body black and blue
It ent have no obeah woman in the world who could concoct a
    cure
    for my kind of Mal Yeux

Blue blue I love you.

Mal Yeux: local term for bad eye, or to look upon someone with evil intent, resulting in a kind of apathethic malaise.

Poyah: East Indian name for machete.

Lalunecowre jouvraway: poet's own bastardisation. French patois, loosely translated to mean: the moon runs her run, but the sun always catches up with her.

J'ouvert: the official opening of Trinidad Carnival from 2a.m. to sunrise. Time of devilish, impish characters. Time for mischief, complete revelry. Also a time for mocking conventions and authority via satire.

Jab jabs: popular impish characters, resembling mud-covered devils, so named for their thrusting, jabbing forks.

Jabmolassie: pretty versions of jab jabs.

Weeping Willow, Jump-up-and-Kiss-me, Stinkin' Susie, Tia Marie: wild flowers.

Phillips Milk of Magnesia bottle: placed in kitchen gardens to repel mal yeux.

Obeah woman: akin to voodoo priestess.

Malika B

Silence is Golden

I did not speak when you burst my beautiful cherry,
by piercing your rod on my butterfly
making the white sheets red
      They called it incest
I did not speak when you speared me
fiery red hot burning pain
      They called it rape
I did not speak when you hit me in my head
      try to make the blue go grey you said
They called it attempted murder
silence is golden, Mama always said,
silence is golden
is gold not precious does it not shine?
is gold not precious does it not shine?
tears cascade inside my silent soul
tortured and tormented
beaten by the licks of life's
bamboo cane blows I remembered
silence is golden, Mama always said,
silence is golden
is gold not precious does it not shine?
is gold not precious does it not shine?

grey matter forms cancer in my silent soul
twisted &
bitter
ranting &
raving
institutionalised &
dehumanised cos
silence is golden, Mama always said,
silence is golden
locked inside drumming over & over
inside my head
gold is precious
gold is precious
gold is precious, why then not am I
gold is precious
gold is precious
gold is precious, why then not am I
thundered out my story
hurricaned out my soul
wailed like a tornado
screeched, shrill NOooooo, NOooooo
as I rocked in this harness
NOooooo, Mama NOooooo
you were wrong so wrong
Noooooo silence is not golden
& institutionalised I shouted out my truth
why   why   why
my butterfly oh free butterfly
red make innocent again

my butterfly oh free butterfly
red make innocent again
but now that I speak
institutionalised no one can hear
Mama is silence golden Mama is silence golden Mama Mama
is silence golden

Shamshad Khan

a day out

i
I am sitting alone today. It is Friday I am feeling low.

ii
The outside of me is clearer than the inside of me the inside has gone gr⊙
and bigger and mouldy.

iii
The sun has not come out for a third day

iv
I am hoping for a look at the sun

v
The warmth on me is making my insides feel more like my outsides

vi
I look in the mirror

vii
I will go out shopping I have looked in the mirror again I have combed m
hair I have got dressed.

viii
I am outside.

Patience Agbabi

Ajax

Just spent my last tenner on white powder, trading
Charles Dickens' crumpled face for a fading

pink postage stamp envelope sealed with a loving kiss.
Supply and demand = business.

OPEN SESAME

Parallel lines deck my mirror,
my destiny mapped out by razor

blade, destination North South
in through the nose, out through the mouth

and it's that ski jump Winter Olympics 78 kick
time is flitting, flying, and it's magic.

My pupils shrink to a fullstop, minute,
my nostrils sprint and my mouth, mute

with soap begins its terrible grinding
dance and I swallow hard like it's a double brandy lining

the inside of the glass like stretch satin,
And I'm Alice, Ali Baba, Aladdin

in the fast lane on the fast stuff.
Don't stop till you get enough.

Time streaks on roller skates faster than a double-decker bus
down streets decked with disco lights, paved with gold dust
to The Underground, the whizz kid's placenta
for the bright lights of the city centre.

OPEN SESAME

I'm devouring the sad ads on the Northbound
till I choke on PENALTY FARE £10

and study the facades on the opposite seat
Trainspotting, Crash and *Deadmeat*

'Fly the tube', I'd rather take a plane
Concorde, to be exact, high on cocaine

'High as a feather boa
70s fashion victim strangles tube controller

for going too slow' that's my mind
working overtime, nose to the grind

and the wages of snorting class ABCs
a) calcium deficiency
b) warped reality
c) split personality

OPEN SESAME

Typical that the doors of perception are jammed
when the queen of the star-studded dance floor's in demand

Time pauses meaningfully, mean
then doors part and time fast forwards, clean
up the down escalator and run
jumps the queue at Club 2001.

OPEN SESAME

They call me Jax, though my real name's Eva
the whole of the Jackson Five rolled into one serious diva

No. 1 on the guest list, top of the charts
when I make my grand entrance, the sea of sequins parts

They're playing *Do What You Wanna Do*, my cue
cos a girl's gotta do what a girl's gotta do

Do The Hustle/Le Freak, says Chic/
Shake your body down to the ground. Then peak.

90s out, 70s in.
dance till our bodies siamese twin.

I take a mammoth dab of uncut paranoia
now I won't speak without a lawyer

and they're playing *Night fever night fever*
from the best disco album in the world, ever

yeah, the Bee Gees are the bee's knees, honey,
Now there goes a man who turns drugs into money

but not tonight, I'm skint and sky high
and on a scale from 'disco' to 'psycho'
I'm 'get out of my fucking space or die'.

Time pulsates at 100 BPM
into the small hours of REM
and the contracted pupils of the chemical class
need to download for the last dance

OPEN SESAME

Open secret. Most of this loo queue have succumbed
to downing uppers, down-in-ones,

don't-look-in-the mirrors and don't-stop-
till-you-get-enoughs. Welcome to the sweet shop

where white light overexposes shady deals
and crisp tenners convert to cheap thrills.

OPEN SESAME

Toilet lid down, the dregs, a thin white line
lines my nostril and drug-fucked I'm bleached clean,
cloned, confused, fused. 5.59.

OPEN SESAME

Time: 6 a.m. Time to unpick
sleep stitched lids. Time to get rich quick
or just get by. Aja, family lawyer from Nigeria,
leaves for her two-pounds-an-hour job as cleaner.

6 a.m. Now 70s chic looks cheap
as I boogie oogie oogie to the beep beep beep

of a space invader machine, worn-out, wide-eyed
my chewing gum long-spun and tumble-dried,

an item of off-white laundry. Time to exit.
Bright light. Day breaks my spirit.

Time: 6.30 a.m. Aja scans the tube ads, prays.
For only God the omnipotent can raise
her spirits in this London, her sugar cane
dreams drowned, choked by cisterns and chains.

OPEN SESAME

And I watch her ascent as I'm coming down,
midway, in this split second, we common ground,

merge, parallel lines, North South, split
personalities, converge, compound, commit.

One way ticket. That's the way I like it.

Lamia Ben Youssef

Ophelia's Soliloquy

To speak, or not to speak, that is the question:
Whether it is chaster to suffer in silence
The pinches of outrageous hoodlums,
Or to take arms against the herd,
And by opposing, castrate them. To speak, to mumble –
No more, and by speaking to say we end
The heartache and the thousand unnatural
Shocks a woman is heiress to.
For who would bear the slings of
The undressing eyes,
The slashes of the wandering hands,
The deaf ears of indifference,
The injustice to the daughter,
The deification of the son,
The misogyny of officialdom,
But that the fearsome mother's
Tool – the poisonous tongue –
Puzzles the will, and makes us rather
Bear those ills we have,
Than rest in the spell of loneliness?
Thus, the fear of Al Razi[1]
Makes silence of us all.

And in this regard, words,
In profound despair,
To our throats retire,
And resting there,
Like worms in a bud,
They feed on the little life left in us.

1. Al Razi is a hospital for the mentally ill in Tunisia.

Joyoti Grech

the last trip

scent of champa
shiuli / rajani gandha
lays its heavy fingers at my table
their names escape me / sweet
music fades the more i
listen / fades
the more i listen /
fades
the more i listen

my house in wreckage
broken and half-broken
possessions washed up in
the hallway / on the landing
loud party booms / i pass through
oblivious / and wary of the danger

in the carpark / searching
the madwoman outside of me
reaches in her coat

good ! i think : a knife/an
end to misery/instead
syringe sprays smack
sends me reeling/panic
focused past the drug
pulls me through / looking for you

back in the broken house
thieves wanking in the doorway
the second stage sets in :
can't hardly walk straight

no vision

the sweet sounds start/fade
the more i listen
fade
the more i listen/fade the more i
listen

reaching for what escapes me:
the end of the trip
pick up the prick of needle tip
something i can handle

reaching

for what escapes me

Kamilah Aisha Moon

Can't Sail The Ocean 'Cause I'm Docked At Cape Fear

Fear is a bully
that shakes me down for confidence
behind the lockers and
demands self-esteem
like milk money
i can only walk on one side of the street
and It always cuts in front of me in line

Fear stalks me like an estranged lover
who refuses to let go
whenever i'm on the verge of giving up potential
to become kinetic
It appears to dredge up old pain
dark moments and every way
that i could possibly fail

how i long to be like my sisters
Wilma outran It into history
dashed right by It
into the heart of a nation
Ella sang It to sleep…then blew It away
in a fierce scat

I bet ol' Mae
laughed all the way to the moon
i pray at night and when the sun
takes her daily stroll
to find the strength said
to lie within us all
and to use it before Fear
takes everything i have
or strangles me
in the heat of the moment

Merle Collins

Hoping

Perhaps if I deliver you my
                                 demon angels
You could move back their folded wings
You might
                    frisk them, touch them, find
the stories their bland angel faces
                                        conceal

Perhaps if I deliver you my
                                 demon angels
You could put laughter in their heaven faces
You might
              touch them, humanize them, find
the hidden spring that holds their
                                      bubbling

Perhaps if I deliver you my
                                 angelic demons
You could bring peace to their restless winging
You might
              humanize them, hold them, still
the thundering that keeps them
                                      moving

Perhaps if I deliver you my
                        demon darkness
You could unfold it, frame it, place it where
the light would touch it, explore it, make a frame
of it, place it where the light would always
                        hold it.

mountain

Jamika Ajalon

when you are poor

steal the cheese
like u usta say
steal the cheese
like ya usta say
sometimes i literally crack
when i can't afford cheese
that's why i said
buy the bread
but steal the cheese
slip it into yr pants
at the back
underneath the coat
& smile – look bored as she rings yr
37p small crusty
wink at the security guard
and slide out the
tescos door
b4 the cheese slips down
past yr buttocks
down yr leg
buy the bread
but steal the cheese

& stretch out your single travel card
across the zonal tube borders
jump the barriers
give yr used ticket to
a ticket tout
on yr way home
go to the bank near closing
and ask for left overs

Lorna Goodison

Tightrope Walker

And I have been a tightrope walker all my life,
that is, tightrope walking has been my main occupation
In between stints in sundry fraudulent circuses
I've worked at poetry, making pictures
or being a paid smart-arse
Once I even tried my hand at cashiering,
couldn't balance the ledger though
but I was honest, always overpaid someone
and had to make up the shortfall myself.
But it was too firm on the ground
so I put on my fishnet tights
my iridescent kingfisher blue bathing-suit
chalked the soles of my slippers of pliable gold kid
and took to the ropes again

It's a fine life, those uncontained moments
in the air
those nerve-stretched belly-bottom spasms
from here to there
and your receiver copping what
from the ground looked like
an innocent feel

as he steadies you safely on the far side.
But I broke both arms
and the side of my head once
and had multiple miscarriages from
falling flat on my back
so I'm on the ground most days now
except for this, the tightest walk of all.
I don my new costume of
marabou and flamingo feathers
and my shade of oyster juliet cap
with the discreet spangles
and inch toward you once or twice a week.
I have to make record time
you have to be home before dark
and the entire act is really a rehearsal
here in this empty tent with last night's
sawdust to buffer the wild in our talk
and the fat lady sunning herself outside
and listening for secrets in our laughter
and it's all done with safety nets, thank you
and no audience invited to the finest
performances of me and you
but it's my life and my last act
before our show closes down
and re-opens to a gaping public
at some other circus ground.

Tired

I am tired
of being tired
I wake up tired
I take my children to school
tired
I go to work
tired
I teach
tired
I pick UP my children from school
tired
I take them to their various after-school activities
tired
I come home
tired
I cook dinner
tired
I help with home-work
tired
I clean up house
tired
I try and get some writing done
tired

I prepare my lesson for teaching
tired
I go to bed
very tired
and before I know it
the alarm clock wakes me up
and I am still tired
I splash water on my face
trying to stir myself
but I am oh so tired
I shower to rejuvenate myself
and just when I think I have licked tired
tired clings to my body in the lotion I rub into it
tired is in the weight of my clothes
tired is my children not wanting to get up
and get dressed for school
tired is me shouting at them to hurry up
tired is me making breakfast
tired is me trying to get us out the house
on time
not too tired or miserable to start the day
tired is me trying not to swear
at the other tired drivers on the freeway
Scram! I shout at tired
but tired just sits there
like a discarded rag
too tired to move
Get a life I yell
but tired is too tired to even care

I try to engage tired in a dialogue
Tired, I say
aren't you tired of always shadowing me
wouldn't you like to visit someone else
but tired is too tired to even respond
Why me I moan
but I am too tired to figure it out
I tell you I am sick and tired
of tired always tiring me out
I am so tired I can't stand myself
and there is no one to complain to
everyone I know is tired of hearing
me say I am tired because they are tired
were tired yesterday
are tired today
would have been tired
have been tired and
will be tired tomorrow
seems like tired
never gets tired
of tiring people out
because I am still tired

Tired is the real name
for working mother

Hope Massiah

New York Nanny

I can only keep doing this job
if I remind myself
that I have a choice,
and a plane ticket in my pocket

I have to remind myself
that I am paid cash
no questions asked,
that I disappear into the ranks of black women
pushing
holding
walking with
white children

I have to remind myself
that I can handle a class full of difficult teenagers
when the five-year-old talks down to me.
I have to remind myself that it isn't servant work
even though it feels like it

I have to remind myself to ignore
the black men who glare at me,
angry that i am
pushing
holding
walking with
white children.
I have to remind myself that
their outrage would disappear,
that I would disappear
if I was
a bit older
a bit darker
a bit bigger

Zebbie Todd

No problem

Me no have no problem.
So how me feel so su su
Me take a day from work
Cause me feel so broke
Ata me parents dem nay
birt me fa turn old mule
And me read say
And hear say slavery
done from when sa
But how come
From morning till night
Me a slave same way
so me slave
so the boss man save

Me no have no problem
Me have big job you know
And I can speaky spoky
Me no dah a bottom
Me deh pon top
Look pon me good
Me have status

House and car
this card and that card
Boy me so credit wordy
Dat anything me see a road
I can take it out pon trust
Wha me so credit wordy
that me nuh need the
Use of money

Wha nay pay out pon dis and dat
Pay out pon bills dem
and every which way me turn
A pure bills dem me buk up pon
If a nuh dat ade pickney dem shoes
mash up
A kick football and anada one
Look like say him mus a de rub
off fe him jacket sleeve
Pon harsh granite wall

Me no have no problem
Cause me have house and car
And big job to top it all
But mind say no badder
Talk dis back
Make I hear say you say
But me have a little cleaning job
Round down suh
Fah when me trash and ready
Nobody nuh dress like me

Man me no have no problem
So how me feel so su su
Ahy sah I think me better
Take anada day from work
Ata me no febah work mule
Shu, you know say
A well time we learn fah rule
A time it now due
It no make no sense
say we a build up dah so call
boss man dem
And dem fake values

Me no have no problem
Africa home de plane
A land
Me will find fah me
owna rank
And deposit
At a fe me owna
Bank.

Maya Angelou

Woman Work

I've got the children to tend
The clothes to mend
The floor to mop
The food to shop
Then the chicken to fry
The baby to dry
I got company to feed
The garden to weed
I've got the shirts to press
The tots to dress
The cane to be cut
I gotta clean up this hut
Then see about the sick
And the cotton to pick.

Shine on me, sunshine
Rain on me, rain
Fall softly, dewdrops
And cool my brow again.

Storm, blow me from here
With your fiercest wind
Let me float across the sky
Till I can rest again.

Fall gently, snowflakes
Cover me with white
Cold icy kisses and
Let me rest tonight.

Sun, rain, curving sky
Mountain, oceans, leaf and stone
Star shine, moon glow
You're all that I can call my own.

fire

Merle Collins

The Sheep and the Goats

this is where you separate the sheep
from the goats

Sometimes
my mother's statements startle
with irrelevance
stay and tickle
disappear to appear again
some unlikely day

Standing in the queue
at the airport terminal
London
Heath-
row

I tried to decide
which were the sheep
and which
the goats

a sudden movement
a twitch
nervous toss of head
to shoulder
a forceful kicking
twitching leg
quick glance through the pages
of a pass-
port
taut tug
at the hand of a fearful child

and
on
the
other
side
the
sheep
serene

a few there
look like us
here
but this is clearly where
you separate
the sheep
from the goats

at the desk
the officer's eyes
proclaim
a cold dislike of goats,
so throats are cleared
for bleating

this is where one begins
to learn
new speaking

when he stamped my pass
I looked down expecting to see
SHEEP

some goats who had tried to wear
sheep's clothing
had been discovered
un-masked
sat silent now along a wall
awaiting return to their pasture

this is where you
separate
the sheep
from the goats

tomorrow
I must write my mother.

they warmakers

words will not stop war
will not stop pain falling
like the sound of your voice
to one who is deaf
and looking another way
lips cannot be read in darkness
in the black sky of nagasaki
death's ray is white and burning
the world where atoms are made
is sacred to those
who no longer guard what they have conquered
who lay their nightmares to rest in clear day
among fields of growing rice
in the hearts of newborns
they waste love
they take and take life
they carry the world into sleep

Pam Ahluwalia

Milk

Milk, she cries;
(no longer mine.)
Now comes from cows,
full fat, semi-skimmed,
condensed in cans.
Cowards!
who slaughter the sacred cow,
whose raging mad disease
is pay back, with infected meat.
Ironic, coincidence or consequence
Natural law, cause and effect.
Causes, project passions
Passion fruit bearing children
And famine, poverty, child slavery
enslaved with denial
hand in hand cuffed. Like convicts
convicted to notions of humanity
humanely calculated on recycled paper
Spread sheets, sheets spread for balancing acts,
death defying acrobats;
milking spectacle,
        sceptical

media reports deity statues are drinking milk.
Ganesh and Laxmi the goddess of wealth
drink until your cows come home.

Stacy Makishi

Spam

I come from a long line of canners.
We canned pineapples. That was our daily grind.
My Uncle Sam canned Spam.
Grinding meat was his daily grind.

My Father said, 'I have no Bikini at all.'
My Mother said, 'You have no Bikini at all.'
My Uncle said, 'There is no Bikini Atoll.'

In 1946 the Yanks dropped a series of nuclear bombs
on an island in the Pacific called Bikini Atoll.
One of the bombs was named 'The Bravo'.
My Uncle said, 'Bravo means, "The opposite of it bombed".'

The Islanders were relocated to where there were no natural
    resources.
But for compensation, the Yanks gave them Spam.

My Uncle decided to change his name,
while the Yanks changed his address,
and renamed him and his wife, Sam and Pam.
My Uncle said, 'We're Sam and Pam. Together we make Spam.'

From *The Happy Isles of Oceania* by Paul Theroux

'It is a theory of mine that former cannibals of Oceania now
feasted on Spam because it came the nearest to approximating
the porky taste of human flesh. They called a cooked human
being 'long pig' in much of Melanesia. It is a fact that the
people-eaters of the Pacific evolved, or perhaps degenerated
into Spam-eaters, because of its corpsey flavour.'

On July 10, 1966
On the bombing anniversary of Bikini Atoll,
Uncle Sam jumped into the meat grinder at Spam.
It was Sam's way of bombing 'em back.

But the Yanks compensated Pam
with 300 cans of Spam.
The cans that might contain Sam.

Akure Wall

Colin Ferguson composed his final
slavery poem in sprayed bullets and
blood on a railroad train floor. post impress-

ionistic gesture? open to interpretation?
explanations – gave not one.
Colin F. mid thirties, angry black male

no more, soared up and left this planet's pain.
self representation at last? – The court room:
take your time. in your own words Mr Blanc,

so what happened next? 'you walked towards me
with your gun raised and shot me three times at
point blank range!'…aaah, can you be sure it was me?

so on to interpret
ation. coon. cocoon. cock.

coon. til the they that is
they see their they in the other

bulls in rings teased with crim-
son things, will gore poor tor-

eadors. and more, sometimes. (op-
en to interpretation…)

we exhibit our symptoms on a stage. speak bitterness, longing and
fury. call

me Malcolm Text. paying jury applauds wildly and in-
vites us back. BRAVO!
ENCORE! more. always more.
all open to interpretation. freedom on HP. a few
more slave narratives to pay and say then I'm free.
but black angst is just
so boring and I'm a song and dance man myself:
slay veree! slay ver ahh!
slay veree! slay ver ah ha ha ha ha ha!
slay veree! slay ver ahh!

that's all folks. thank you very much for coming
out, you've been a
delightful audience. hope you
enjoyed the show. if you did please tell your
friends. If not I dare you to tell me. travel safe. good night.
God bless.

Karen McCarthy

The Last Slavery Poem…

The thunderous sky sweats her bloody child
Watch the bodies drop, flip flop; arms, legs: limbs
Piled high. Eye screwed tight, clenched against the pain

A burning, bitter, deadly acid rain.
Dis-figuring, dis-colouring, just plain
dis-stressing, the soft, brown skin of the earth.

Time and time again. Memories flik-flak
Back and back, backs broken, hearts broken. Child
Taken. The newborn stillborn. But there is

Still some breath – some life in the ancient in-
fant yet. Backs broken, hearts aching. Child taken.
But spirit still strong, still strong. Spirit still strong.

To be unbreakable
would seem impossible

Can't break me in, or out
of my mind, which will fight

To the bitterest end.
The beginning only

A part of the story
Not every child must die.

Jean 'Binta' Breeze

Mother…Sister…Daughter

If you should see me,
walking down the street,
mouth muffled
head low against the wind,
know
that this is no woman bent
on sacrifice
just
heavy
with the thoughts
of freedom…

Samantha Coerbell

womb envy

this is one of those barren times when
what goes on beyond the fire escape
doesn't matter
born are the babies with veins of steel
holding strongly onto the sins of their fathers
carriages rumble through the street
with little girl-mothers pushing themselves
into a life that really may never be
it doesn't matter really
it couldn't possibly
if i think of one of those people
sitting in my living room
sipping chamomile tea
eating biscuits
it wouldn't be possible to force out the words
that need to pass between us
she could never explain the gold on her arm
and the lack of a bank account
i can't describe why i don't think about tomorrow
i am planning my death
i say i will die next year/month/week
this is a happy thing

in my contemplation
she tells me she doesn't think of death
it is manifest
she does not ponder much
there are bills piling in her corner of no where
her children are hungry
frequently feasting on 25 cent drinks
and on the forgotten remainders of time
she cannot teach them to reach beyond herself
because she does not care to learn how
i envy her
wanting to drag my brood through the street
battling the current of oppression
a force i don't really feel the weight of
not the way it is described in text books
the lumpenproletariat should rise up
and i think hey, that's me
i'm just too tired to lift myself to the sink
this is just going to be one of those days
where everything falls into the center
manoeuvred by an unseen hand
i voted in the last election and thought
it mattered if clinton gave out the welfare checks
instead of george bush
staring at the woman across the divide
she could have told me i was wrong to care
but i didn't think to ask her
the days are too busy for chamomile tea
and biscuits with unknown women

all i want is to make my way through the streets
unscathed. childless. man-free. spirited.
we may not be that different.
maybe i think too much.
don't just go and live.
can't seem to do.
enough of me.
look at her
don't you
want to
be like
her.

Nikki Giovanni

I Laughed When I Wrote It
(Don't You Think It's Funny?)

the f.b.i. came by my house three weeks ago
one white agent one black (or i guess negro would be
more appropriate) with two three-button suits on (one to a man)
thin ties – cuffs in the bottoms – belts at their waists
they said in unison:

    ms giovanni you are getting to be quite important

    people listen to what you have to say

i said nothing

    we would like to have to give a different message

i said: gee are all you guys really shorter than hoover
they said:

    it would be a patriotic gesture if you'll quit saying

    you love rap brown and if you'd maybe give us some leads

    on what some of your friends are doing

i said: fuck you
a week later the c.i.a. came by two unisexes one blond afro
one darker one three bulges on each showing lovely bell-

    bottoms and boots

they said in rounds:

    sister why not loosen up and turn on

    fuck the system up from the inside

    we can turn you on to some groovy

>trips and you don't have to worry
>about money or nothing   take the commune
>way and a few drugs it'll be good for you
>and the little one

after i finished a long loud stinky fart i said serenely
definitely though with love
>fuck you

yesterday a representative from interpol stopped me in the
  park
tall. neat afro, striped hip huggers bulging only in the right
  place
>i really dig you. he said. i want to do something for you
>and you alone

i asked what he would like to do   for me
>need a trip around the world a car bigger apartment
>are you lonely i mean we need to get you comfortable
>cause a lot of people listen to you and you
>need to be comfortable to put forth a positive image

and digging the scene i said listen i would sell
out but i need to make it worth my while you understand
>you just name it and i'll give it to you, he assured me

well. i pondered, i want aretha franklin and her piano
>reduced to fit next to my electric

typewriter on my desk and i'll do anything you want
he lowered his long black eyelashes and smiled a whimsical
  smile
>fuck you. nikki. he said

[7 jan 72]

Sujata Bhatt

Frauenjournal

A woman kills
her newborn granddaughter
because she has four already.

A woman kills because
there's not enough money
not enough milk.

A woman kills her newborn daughter
and still eats dinner
and still wears a green sari.

Is this being judgemental?
Or is this how one bears witness
                    with words?

And another woman in another country
makes sure that her seven-year-old daughter
has her clitoris sliced off
with a razor blade.
This is what they will show us
tonight – prime time –

We're advised not to let our children watch this.
This has never been filmed before.
Sometimes it's necessary
to see the truth. The moderator tells us
words are not enough.

Now the camera focuses on
the razor blade – so there is no doubt
about the instrument. The razor blade
                              is not a rumour.

Now the camera shifts over
to the seven-year-old face:
she smiles – innocent – she doesn't know.
The girl smiles – she feels important.
And then the blood and then the screams.

Why do I think I have to watch this?
Is this being a voyeur?
Or is this how one begins
to bear witness?

And another woman tells us how years ago
she accidentally killed her own daughter
while trying to cut out her clitoris.
The risks are great, she tells us,
but she's proud of her profession.

How much reality can you bear?

And if you are a true poet
why can't you cure

                anything with your words?

The camera focused
long and steady on the razor blade.
At least it wasn't rusty.

How can you bear witness
with words how can you heal

                anything with words?

The camerawoman could not
afford to tremble or flinch.
She had to keep a steady hand.
And the hand holding the razor blade
did not hesitate.

And if you are a true poet
will you also find a voice
for the woman who can smile
after killing her daughter?

What is the point of bearing witness?

Afterwards, the girl can barely walk.

For days the girl will hobble – unable
unable unable

unable to return
to her old self,
her old childish way of life.

Jayne Cortez

Global Inequalities

Chairperson of the board
is not digging for roots
    in the shadows
There's no dying-of-hunger stare
    in eyes of
Chief executive officer of petroleum
Somebody else is sinking into
    spring freeze of the soil
Somebody else is evaporating
    in dry wind of the famine
there's no severe drought
    in mouth of
Senior vice president of funding services
No military contractor is sitting
    in heat of a disappearing lake
No river is drying up
    in kidneys of
    a minister of defense
Under-secretary of interior
    is not writing distress signals
    on shithouse walls
Do you see refugee camp cooped up

in head of
Vice president of municipal bonds
There's no food shortage
in belly of
a minister of agriculture
Chief economic advisors are
addicted to diet pills
Banking committee members are
suffering from obesity
Somebody else is sucking on dehydrated nipples
Somebody else is filling up on fly specks
The Bishops are not
forcing themselves to eat bark
The security exchange commission members
are sick from
too many chocolate chip cookies
The treasury secretary
is not going around in circles
looking for grain
There's no desert growing in nose of
Supreme commander of justice
It's somebody else without weight
without blood without land
without a cloud cover of water on the face
It's somebody else
Always somebody else

air

Jayne Cortez

Samba is Power

In Brazil
I sambaed on the road to Joa Pesoa
I sambaed on the beach of transparent crabs
I sambaed to sounds of iron bells
in State of Bahia
I sambaed while eating muqueca
while watching capoiera
while wearing Oxum belt made by
maker of ritual objects in Salvador
I sambaed through São Paulo airport
sambaed into dark-skin light-skin African
Indian Portuguese situations of struggle
I sambaed into translations while drinking batidas
with writers at Eboni Bookstore
I sambaed while waiting for a short mustached
so-called mulatto who swore
he was a Yoruba Babalawo I sambaed
I sambaed onto corner of handcuffed
Afro-Brazilian men
sambaed next to women who were
spinning pulsating & assaulting police cars
I sambaed into house of condomble

into congress of Black culture
Into Perfil of African Literature
I sambaed
I sambaed next to the red buildings of Exu
I sambaed with Ge Ge & Egbas
I sambaed into trance of Yemaya
I sambaed with Oko
I sambaed in front of the daughters of Santos
I sambaed against walls of political graffiti
I sambaed with Shango
I sambaed with Mai do Samba
My samba wrapped in orisha ribbons
my samba mixed with human smells & feijoada
my samba infused with vatapa & caprinhas
the up hill samba bursting out of my feet
the samba whistles hollering out of my navel
the samba fetishes buzzing high
in sambadome of my soul
as I sambaed & sambaed & sambaed & sambaed
I sambaed diagonally through Recife floods
sambaed upward through steel cages of Brasilia
sambaed away from alcohol fumes
in Copacabana
sambaed behind homeless children
with soccer ball eyes
sambaed past dealers dealing drugs
sambaed into costume room
in communedado Mangueira
sambaed in front of protestant missionaries

who preached that samba is sin
but samba is life
samba is friction
samba is power
& I sambaed & sambaed & sambaed
sambaed into circles with Rei Mo Mo
as he shook his heavy flesh in slow motion
sambaed next to young women quivering
their brown calves in quadruple time
my samba getting drunk off the high speed rhythms
my samba embedded with bass drums of cachca
my samba parading & scorching teeth of
the Rio de Janeiro sun
my samba absorbing the forest stench
of poet from Amazonas
my samba squatting down & wiggling up
as I sambaed the samba of my memory
the samba of my fantasy
the samba of my samba
because samba is life
samba is friction
samba is power
samba is everything
that's why I sambaed & sambaed & sambaed

Amiti Grech

Roots

I am my roots,
I replied
to his query.
I carry all the seasons.
The oriole calls
in the valley,
the hills keep the echoes.
The eternal in me
rests in the hills,
lifts in the air
with kingfisher and oriole.
The wind bending
the rice-paddy
touched my cheeks first.
The river swelling in the rains
flowed through my growth.
The mould of my thoughts,
the shape of my speech
have been formed
by a sky dark with July,
deep with December blue.

Lisa Asagi

A Small Film

In the film of this flight, the screen is small and painted with moving cells.

It is a movie of a dying star, who in her last millennium still found
a way to help a soul
locate itself

In the gravity of amassing days, in the confusion
of disappearing nights, the film unrolls
in flickered silence

and waits to be rewound. Over and over again, she walks
into the room. She walks into the room and becomes
the one who bears the lines.

The crevices exist from what is not said. Around her
are ravines of these things, threads strung tight, as she walks
across the softness of bent cellulose.

The person who watches is awakened at night. Sees her walk off the
    building
of a dream and tries to stop her. She cannot tell anyone why this
    memory will exist.

The watcher is the dreamer who whispers,
how you stand on a balcony from yet another island.

In recesses beneath streets of strange cities, this dream
will always unfold. In songs of unknown tongues
it is conjured, in bottles of wine slightly turned
by conflicts of weather, like bones found
on the bank of a cold river.
A sunken tomb emerges
in a dervish of warm water
within a chilled body,
and asks if there is
something more
to remember.

In an absence left
for remembrance.

In cells of skin left behind.

In the smallness of a back
in a very far night.

Lorna Goodison

Some of My Worst Wounds

Some of my worst wounds
have healed into poems
A few well placed
stabs in the back
have released a singing
trapped between my shoulders.
A carrydown
has lent leverage
to the tongue's rise
and betrayals sent words
hurrying home
to toe the line again.

City Blues

1. The Wolf (at the door)

Because my mind is troubled
It's difficult to sink
Into the patchwork frame
Of sleep.

I lie half-draped
Across the bed
Having yawned through a chapter
Or two
And – still dressed
Face unwashed –
Never even go to sleep
Properly.

Afraid
Of the wolf at the door
The distant knock
The seafried hopes
The earthen jar
The globe-shaped pot

Morning comes
Too soon – and I
Must get up and get
But so faint-hearted
Afraid that I might slip
And fall
Tired of trying and all that
And there's no home
Because I haven't built it yet…

2. Blind Alley

Despair is a thief
In time's blind alley
And after the farewell
What I've found is:
Romance stays.

Wild music – an insistent
Relentless Chopin
Gypsy forays
Dangerous rocks
Crashing waves, wind
Passion and sin
And all that stuff.
And why the hell not?
Them who's careful
Remain well cared for

But them who risk
Don't always
End up broke.

3. Route 1

I cannot explaln
Why I chose
The dangerous route
When I love the safe one
So weary

Every Christmas
I set out
Hearts alight
Flags unfurled
Popcorn strings, HOME
To have myself
A merry little Christmas

Safety…
But the other life
Is hard and alone
I never chose it
Just knew it
When it met me
As one meets something
Anything
Along the road

So all the circles of home
Firelight, lamplight
Bone tiredness and rest
May warm
For a time
And always, must leave
Finding the voices
To carry me
Into the bitterwind

What lives and loves
And no shelter
And knowing where to go
I would...I would

4. Route II

I travelled the morning sun
My harbour –
Only brown arms sinewy
And full of healing –
Leaving this,
No visions in sight
Leaving the green-bushed hills,
A sea of sadness
Coral-gripped, flailing
Anemones royal-blue
Trailing veins of old
Unsettled blood

God what is the terror
Which grips me to the core
And blinds the running
Sea-sucked eye
Of the old one who sees

I am become Tiresias
And can see everything
And feel it all
And no relief in sight…

5. The Word

I sit alone
In a still house

All my familiars have gone
And no dear ghosts
Return to warm
Their still, cold hands

Thrown upon
Myself
At last:

In fear and trembling
Lacerated with tears
My dear false friend
– An unknown muse –
Cradling me

Know
I must bring
To birth – my word –
Dread or otherwise
To light.

Sujata Bhatt

Swami Anand

In Kosbad during the monsoons
there are so many shades of green
your mind forgets other colours.

At that time
I am seventeen, and have just started
to wear a sari every day
Swami Anand is eighty-nine
                and almost blind.
His thick glasses don't seem to work,
they only magnify his cloudy eyes
Mornings he summons me
     from the kitchen
and I read to him until lunch time

One day he tells me
'you can read your poems now'
I read a few, he is silent.
Thinking he's asleep, I stop.
But he says, 'continue'.
I begin a long one
in which the Himalayas rise
                as a metaphor.

Suddenly I am ashamed
to have used the Himalayas like this,
ashamed to speak of my imaginary mountains
to a man who walked through
      the ice and snow of Gangotri
         barefoot
a man who lived close to Kangchenjanga
    and Everest clad only in summer cotton.
I pause to apologize
but he says 'just continue'.

Later, climbing through
     the slippery green hills of Kosbad,
Swami Anand does not need to lean
on my shoulder or his umbrella.
I prod him for suggestions,
ways to improve my poems.
He is silent a long while,
then, he says
     'there is nothing I can tell you
        except continue.'

elemental

Sujata Bhatt

અેડલી (Udaylee)*

Only paper and wood are safe
from a menstruating woman's touch.
So they built this room
for us, next to the cowshed.
Here, we're permitted to write
letters, to read, and it gives a chance
for our kitchen-scarred fingers to heal.

Tonight, I can't leave the stars alone.
And when I can't sleep, I pace
in this small room, I pace
from my narrow rope-bed to the bookshelf
filled with dusty newspapers
held down with glossy brown cowries and a conch.
When I can't sleep, I hold
the conch shell to my ear
just to hear my blood rushing,
a song throbbing,
a slow drumming within my head, my hips.
This aching is my blood flowing against,
rushing against something
knotted clumps of my blood,

so I remember fistfuls of torn seaweed
          rising with the foam,
rising. Then falling, falling up on the sand
strewn over newly laid turtle eggs.

* અડલી (Udaylee): untouchable when one is menstruating

Opal Palmer Adisa

Full of Herself

Moon has always known
what she wants
and how to get it
No obstacle can keep her back
Her will defies
all boundaries

Confident and self-assured
she works diligently
to achieve what she wants
She is not a fickle woman
Her heart meets the homeless
and offers them comfort
She guides the lonely traveler
Her smile serves as inspiration
to writers
She likes company
and wherever she travels
her admirers dazzle the galaxy
but she radiates more brilliantly
awakening the entire sky
with her full-faced laughter.

Sharan Strange

The Stranger

The one I like most is about her – a story with so few details it became mystery, with so few versions it remains myth. This much I can tell you. She was married, had a family. I know this because her granddaughter-in-law told the story to her daughter, who told it to me. What was she like? I picture her small and lean, brown as pines, with hair like bare branches in winter. Did she grow very old? How did she die? None of this I know, only that she was a dark woman from South Carolina. And she was unpredictable.

She'd come and go as the spirit moved her, disappearing for days without a word. It wasn't a lover who lured her, or a craving for adventure – that was common as dirt yards in those parts. No, it was a calling, a witnessing she had to do. . . Eventually, not even her husband dared question her. Like the others, he simply waited for her return, waited to see if she had changed. But she didn't appear changed. Only something slight, dimly perceived, hovered about her, like the first glimmerings of new light after the passing of a storm.

Nothing more could be said about her – yes, she could heal them with her roots and leaves. And she could read their dreams. After a time, they grew used to her wanderings. But who wouldn't be intrigued when she came home after a week in the woods, barefoot, with a bag of live snakes, a pale mark blooming on her forehead, and some strange landscape hinted at in her eyes?

That is the truth as it was passed on to me. Did it happen? Who can say. I ponder this sliver of a tale, and her ways, which seem to me those of a wisewoman or shaman. Then there is the real story, the one no one can tell me: what happened in those woods. Half-a-life and no-name, she has been given to me. I come back to her often, gazing in the mirror at a face with its own wild luminance, its own secrets.

Phenomenal Woman

Pretty women wonder where my secret lies.
I'm not cute or built to suit a fashion model's size
But when I start to tell them,
They think I'm telling lies.
I say,
It's in the reach of my arms,
The span of my hips,
The stride of my step,
The curl of my lips.
I'm a woman
Phenomenally.
Phenomenal woman,
That's me.

I walk into a room
Just as cool as you please,
And to a man,
The fellows stand or
Fall down on their knees.
Then they swarm around me,
A hive of honey bees.

I say,
It's the fire in my eyes,
And the flash of my teeth,
The swing in my waist,
And the joy in my feet.
I'm a woman
Phenomenally.
Phenomenal woman,
That's me.

Men themselves have wondered
What they see in me.
They try so much
But they can't touch
My inner mystery.
When I try to show them,
They say they still can't see.
I say,
It's in the arch of my back,
The sun of my smile,
The ride of my breasts,
The grace of my style.
I'm a woman
Phenomenally.
Phenomenal woman,
That's me.

Now you understand
Just why my head's not bowed.
I don't shout or jump about
Or have to talk real loud.
When you see me passing,
It ought to make you proud.
I say,
It's in the click of my heels,
The bend of my hair,
the palm of my hand,
The need for my care.
'Cause I'm a woman
Phenomenally.
Phenomenal woman,
That's me.

Dorothea Smartt

five strands of hair

*'As a Black person and a woman I don't read history for
facts. I read it for clues"*

Alice Walker, *Elle*, October, 1989, p45

i. parting

I began clenched teeth.
Tight steel combs, and
mother's fingers –
slippery Dax heroines,
pulled out the need.

Plaited and stocking-capped,
beside her head
the pungent edge of frying hair
smoked brown-paper twists,
greased and combed;
prevention is better than cure.

ii. clueless

Her hair is straight
no twists or crosses

a wiped clean page
it doesn't read.

curled out
no markers to ancestry –

> that we have bad hair
> that we have coolie in the family
> that it tough and don't grow – no

see
her hair it's straight.
it doesn't read
easy.

iii. twists and turns

Fact:
1. Your hair is an integral part of your skin.
2. There is good hair, there is bad hair.
3. Hair and scalp diseases were common among enslaved Africans.
4. A chemical used to straighten African hair is called 'lye'.
5. Natural African hair must be processed to make it manageable.
6. Black women spend a major part of their income fixing their hair.
7. Straightening hair made the first US Black millionairess.
8. Black women need the hairdresser more often than white women.
9. Different styles of plaiting and braiding marked rites of passage.
10. Unkempt hair is a sign of madness.

iv. a foreign head

She fetched
all through Sunday-best dinner.
Twisting and looking
the question hovered round.
A well-raised Bajan girl,
she was too-too polite,
until outside bursting she could
ask mummy-friend bigwoman dawter –
'you is a rasta?!'

v. revert

Still shouldering a Black Star Line,
he said no –
'doan vex the children hair with foolishness.'
His own balding masthead,
crowned with ancient mystery books.
The deep science
of pale-faded Egyptians –
the African headdress
(be)stowed away on me.

Dana Marrett-Silvera

Silent Talking

I didn't talk much today.
Those who did all the talking kept asking
'are you okay?'
Kept asking 'why are you so quiet?'
In my head I answered…

There is power in silence.
There is strength in silence.
There is learning in silence.
There is renewal in silence.
There is solitude and safety in silence.

There is hearing in silence.
There is healing in silence.
There is knowing in silence.
There is mystery in silence
     and mysteries are solved in silence.

There is peace in silence.
There is grief in silence.
There is growth in silence.
There is hope in silence.

There are dreams in silence.
There is creativity in silence.
There is music and madness in silence.

There is vision in silence.
There is joy in silence.
There are words and sentences,
and chapters and books, in silence.

There is insight in silence.
There is passion in silence.
There is fantasy in silence.
There is love in silence.
There are memories in silence.
There is movement and rhythm
and colour, in silence.

There is breath in silence.
There is life and death in silence.

Sometimes my spirit leads me into silence.
I dare to embrace it.
If you need to question it.
I will answer.
In silence.

Alice Walker

A Woman is not a Potted Plant

her roots bound
to the confines
of her house

a woman is not
a potted plant
her leaves trimmed
to the contours
of her sex

a woman is not
a potted plant
her branches
espaliered
against the fences
of her race
her country
her mother
her man

her trained blossom
turning

this way
& that
to follow
the sun
or whoever feeds
and waters
her

a woman
is wilderness
unbounded
holding the future
between each breath
walking the earth
only because
she is free
and not creepervine
or tree.

Nor even honeysuckle
or bee.

Rosamond S King

She be

She begets the heaven and the earth.

She begets lightness and darkness and the day and the night.

She begets optics.

She begets water and land and the plants.

She begets ecology and botany.

She begets the stars and the planets.

She begets astronomy.

She begets the animals and fish and fowl.

She begets biology.

She begets woman in Her image and

She begets a man.

She be gettin got by Her mother, who forgot to tell Her this.

She be gettin got by some man who didn't know either and now

She be gettin got with children with no daddy but before this

She be gettin got by burnt out teachers in schools with no windows
   and no books and now

She be gettin got by the j-o-b with no m-o-n-e and

She be gettin got by credit and

She be gettin got by the rent for this room and

She be gettin got by the lady selling cosmetics and

She be gettin got by religion.

She be gettin got by the forgetting in forgot.

She be gettin got by getting got by not getting and
She be gettin got by Herself. But
She be gettin up now.
She be gettin up out of Herself in order that
She be gettin up out of the forgetting and that
She be gettin up out of the forgot.
She be stripping the leaves off of isms and obias.
She be scattering them under Her feet.
She be breathing deep.
She be spreading out Her fissssssssst.
She be She be She be She be looking at Her daughter.
She be the heaven and the earth and the lightness of darkness
    and the day and the night.
She be the water and the land and all the living things.
She be woman in Her image.
She be

circle

Rachel Manley

Memoryectomy

Part by part
appears to be working so well,
and yet there's a falling apart…
no, not falling…
nor is anything
torn asunder or pulled;
rather, pruned neatly,
stripped clean of the binding
of frayed, dried leaves
that composts…
cleverly lanced scars:
a memoryectomy.

But keloids
were all little voices
that told tales in the dark
of triumphs;
ragged battle flags,
tiny In Requiems
saluting old pain,
bundled headstones
with their quotations.

Now they bloom
without the message
of scent.

Parm Kaur

Wiping the wall

I add bleach to the sponge
to wipe clean the bathroom wall
of rot inducing spores.

If only bleach could be drunk
the body cleansed as easily.

Mozart's finely wrought piano pieces
spawn shafts which reach around the open door
to pierce the skin, pricking buried sores.

'He missed the heat,' his wife said. He missed it again
as his ashes were tipped, as one he hit the fast
flowing river in the pink grey chill of dawn.

She laughed after bathing in the same cold river
finally free of his last wish, to be returned.

Did damp English winters and ways induce organs
inside to grow coats of fur to warm, or was it
the blood that rose like poisoned sap to stop his heart?

She cannot laugh now, or sob. Her face bloats, a fish belly
up in the water, eyes dribbling. She has to keep it
in, together, must, can't, have to, for the children.

For an instant I see him again as
I want to, on the bathroom wall, laughing.

Amy Ling

Fragile

Like well-trained ants we go our chosen way,
following a trail some dim ancestor lay
from home to tree and back again to hole
carrying our piece of leaf, life's only goal,
falling in line, antennae never still
not to lose that trail back to the hill
unaware that some sudden blue afternoon
a callous, careless sole would just as soon
as kick a stone, crush out our lives, confuse
the trail, topple our ordered home, refuse
to care about compartments for the queen,
the workers; like a flash that's barely seen
everything slowly built can quickly die
as oaks upturned by lightning from the sky
when crazed assassins shoot a president,
a singing star his life only half spent,
Atlanta's children murdered when they roam
and cancer strikes a cousin close to home.
So occupied are we, we don't intend
to think on what slight threads our lives depend.

Kamilah Aisha Moon

For Whom the Phone Rings

it happens at least a dozen times a day
friends, lovers, telemarketers
shady credit card deals
but today I heard the shrill pitch
as if for the first time
noted the two-second pause between each
electric scream
the halting hello after trembling fingers
answer the call
the era of modern technology spawned
the machine that found the mass
not yet discernible by touch and
the phone line that carried the news
sorry Mrs Moon, it is not benign
fate transmitted in milliseconds courtesy of AT&T
helplessness settles on me like morning dew on the shrubs
that border our house
mutant cells threaten to steal my Mama from me
and the most I can do is help her cry
continue to offer prayers that appear
to have been denied
to be there when she must sacrifice her remaining mound of flesh

that outwardly symbolizes her womanhood
a devastating thing in our cosmo society
where cleavage often equals clout
and we're constantly fed that T & A is what
being a woman is all about
I must witness her painful farewell to breasts
that sprouted when Motown was born
tantalized her new husband when afros were thick and long
comforted napping children while OPEC was going on
so this is what it feels like at ground zero
when it is no longer just the housewife from Fresno
Ann Jillian's made-for-TV movie
the 1 in 9 statistic quoted in PSAs on the radio
although folks go to Lotto
to play the odds
this number she never wanted to hit once
but decided to strike twice
it's so damn unfair
Mama's already seen the drain clogged
by her own hair
I hope this time isn't too much to bear
we love, need and want her
too soon to part company now
I want my children to hear Grandma read
The Little Engine That Could and exclaim WOW
another thought occurs and
it makes me feel ashamed
watching her pain and anguish
20 years from now

I could feel the same
Mama, Mama
you've got to make it through…

those rings sounded like a C sharp
1 thousand 1, 1 thousand 2

Honor Ford-Smith

Dinner at the Apartment in Toronto

Silence
is the web encircling us,
noisy as the clanging of washed pots
or the bawling of a cow butchered in the hills.

Discharged from hospital you are sitting
on a couch in a highrise in Toronto.
I sit resentfully opposite looking at you
locked, like Frida Kahlo, in your iron spinal brace
the plastic clasp cutting through the thin flesh
covering your heart. Through the glass
a white sheet covers the city's winter body.

I have stopped work and come here to take care of you.
You're glad I'm here. You want me with you.
I want to get away.   You smile at me.   You plan dinner.
You make dinner.   For though I know I should
I am used to the habit of your taking charge,
accustomed to deferring to your power,
We sit at the table set for the dinner rite
and chew chicken, rice and the obligatory salad in silence

You have shrunk seven inches in two months since your spine
   collapsed.
Your ribs splinter each time you stretch.
You never complain, never speak of death or the God you pray to
though the invocation of heavenly intervention is evident
in the tracts from 'Unity' and 'The Daily Word' beside your bed.

Your disease has rotted my soldier crab's shell
and I am shocked to want what I have condemned.
I inventory my could-have-beens:
a gun toting stockbroking BMW driving husband,
a four bedroom house in Norbrook with two starched helpers,
a gardener, security guard. A proper job. And vicious dogs.
What else? A gate that throws its arms open at one touch
of my manicured finger to the remote. A flat for you
to live in, devoted grandchildren and a nurse.
These things will never be. This is the end of that,
and I swallow a piece of lettuce and tomato.

You were as I was always told, an anomaly in your time
a woman doctor, single mother, single island scholar,
singular educated woman of colour. Now you are counting
all you were not, as you swallow the rice grains
I see you examining the failed marriages
the effort not to be so distant, to express yourself,
to be ordinary, a middle class woman with a home,
a nuclear family, a love of gossip or dancing,
a wife who tolerates a womanizing husband for the sake of three

children, who sublimates humiliation in church work perhaps,
or embroiders in an armchair by a window.
Those discarded choices have long been dumped or burned.

We have only what has been: the silence and
the loud words thrown like cutlasses across the yard
the jealousies, each other's oppositions,
stalemates and the unresolved differences,
the secrets – shards enmeshed in the web
encircling us – these discontinuities of love.
Dinner is over. We are clearing the table now.

Janet Kofi-Tsekpo

The Garden

Blood exiled from the heart
is old and hard. Blackberry clumps

drop on to the lawn patch
where my grandfather's hairs

stray among the yellowing grass,
as she snips and I pick,

feeling the soft flesh burst its blood
on my hands. 'Thank you, dear.'

He smiles white ivory,
the mirror shining in

all the right places, the
big scissors wincing in the sun.

We sip insipid tea
to unclog the chocolate roll now

well past the sell-by date,
and avert our eyes from

that huge boil setting west. It falls
hard from the weeping light.

Plants

Plants are deceptive. You see them there
looking as if once rooted they know
their places; not like animals, like us
always running around, leaving traces.

Yet from the way they breed (excuse me!)
and twine, from their exhibitionist
and rather prolific nature we must infer
a sinister not to say imperialistic

grand design. Perhaps you've regarded,
as beneath your notice, armies of mangrove
on the march, roots in the air, clinging
tendrils anchoring themselves everywhere?

The world is full of shoots bent on conquest,
invasive seedlings seeking wide open spaces,
materiel gathered for explosive dispersal
in capsules and seed cases.

Maybe you haven't quite taken in the
colonizing ambitions of hitchhiking
burrs on your sweater, surf-riding nuts
bobbing on ocean, parachuting seeds and other

airborne traffic dropping in. And what
about those special agents called flowers?
Dressed, perfumed, and made-up for romancing
insects, bats, birds, bees, even you –

– don't deny it, my dear, I've seen you
sniff and exclaim. Believe me, Innocent,
that sweet fruit, that berry, is nothing
more than ovary, the instrument to seduce

you into scattering plant progeny. Part of
a vast cosmic program that once set
in motion cannot be undone though we
become plant food and earth wind down.

They'll outlast us, they were always there
one step ahead of us: plants gone to seed,
generating the original profligate,
extravagant, reckless, improvident, weed.

Raman Mundair

Nāātch

Dancing on broken glass like Pakeezah,
blood trickling from my mehndied feet
judgemental voyeuristic eyes
Watch me
chākar after chākar
I spin as if I alone hold
the axle of the world
in the balance of my heels
as my toes touch shards of broken remnants of hope
I take the weight
and I weave it into the momentum of
my sufi, khatak, flamenco
Nāātch.

Nāātch: (Panjabi, Hindi, Urdu) dance
Pakeezah: fictional female Hindi film character now an icon. In the
    film of the same name Pakeezah dances on broken glass in order
    to prove her honour. Pakeezah literally translates as 'pure of
    heart'.
Mehndi: henna designs worn in celebration at religious festivals and
    marriage ceremonies.
Chākar: a graceful khatak spin of 6/8 beats per second. Can also
    mean a long, weary journey or a rut.
Khatak: classical north-Indian dance form.

Biographical Notes

Opal Palmer Adisa is a Jamaican-born literary critic, poet, prose writer and storyteller. Her published works include *It Begins With Tears* (1997) and *Tamarind and Mango Women* (1992), which won the PEN Oakland/Josephine Miles Award. Her work has been anthologised in many collections, including *Sisterfire: Black Womanist Fiction and Poetry* (The Women's Press, 1995), and *Creation Fire: A CAFRA Anthology of Caribbean Women's Poetry* (1990). She is currently Associate Professor and Chair of the Ethnic Studies Programme at California College of Arts and Crafts. She lives in Oakland California, where she is raising her three children.

Patience Agbabi is a London-based internationally renowned performance poet. In 1997 she won the Excelle Literary Award for poetry and joined the London Arts Board Literature Advisory Group. She is especially inspired by rap and poetry that takes risks in form or content. Her first collection, *R.A.W.* was published in 1995, and in 1998 three of her poems were featured in Channel 4's *Litpop* performance poetry series. Agbabi is currently working solo and is enjoying putting together her second poetry collection.

Pam Ahluwalia worked as a community development officer and voluntary sector trainer for ten years before embarking on a writing career. She gained a degree in writing and publishing at Middlesex University and has since helped to form Roti Writers, a writers' group for people of Asian origin, of which she is now Chairperson. She has performed at a number of events and venues, including storytelling at the Bollywood Bazaar, part of Channel 4's 50th Anniversary Celebrations of India's independence, and has appeared at the Poetry Cafe. She is moving into the narrative genre and is currently working on a novel and a series of inteviews with black writers exploring their work and process.

Jamika Ajalon was born in St Louis and studied at the University of Missouri; at Columbia, Missouri; and then Chicago, where she received a BA in Film. Jamika became particularly involved in the 'divest from South Africa' movement. She went on to travel round the States before coming to London, where she studied at Goldsmiths and was awarded an MA in Cultural Theory & Media. Jamika is currently working on a novel, *Alien-nation*, and a proposal for an anthology. As a performance poet, Jamika has appeared with the Urban Poets in the UK and at venues in Chicago and New York. She has written for various publications, including the *Black Book Review* (NY) and the *BFI Black Film Bulletin*. Jamika has made several short films, including *Blood Poem, Intro to Cultural Skitzofrenia, Shades* and *Memory Tracks*, and has created various video-poetry installations. Her current projects include working with Cultural Partnerships Production Company on a project about the history of Black and Jewish settlement in Britain.

Maya Angelou has been a waitress, singer, actress, dancer, activist, editor, filmmaker, writer, mother, and now inaugural poet. She first thrilled the world with *I Know Why the Caged Bird Sings* which forms the first instalment of her famous five-part autobiography. She has also written several collections of poetry: *And Still I Rise, Just Give Me a Cool Drink of Water 'Fore I Die* and *I Shall Not Be Moved*, all of which are featured in *The Complete Collected Poems*. In 1993 Maya Angelou wrote her historic poem *On the Pulse of Morning*, for the inauguration of President Clinton. She now has a lifetime appointment as Reynolds Professor of American Studies at Wake Forest University, North Carolina.

Lisa Asagi was born on the island of Oahu, Hawaii. Currently residing in San Francisco, she is researching and writing a novel-length manuscript entitled *Isola*.

Malika B is a British born writer of Caribbean descent, hailing from a Grenadian mother and a Guyanese father. She spent 13 years of her childhood in Guyana, a time she attests to being the best years of her life. She has performed with many writers including sapphire, Terry McMillan and Earl Lovelace. A former member of the Mannafest Collective, Malika has recorded work for BBC Radio 4 and is featured on the *Tongue & Groove* poetry compilation album. She is now Education Worker for the poetry agency Apples & Snakes and has facilitated workshops and lectures for North London University, Goldsmiths College, Oval House Theatre, and Greenwich International Festivals and presently teaches a performance poetry course for Hackney College.

Chitra Banarjee Divakaruni, born in India, is an award-winning poet who teaches creative writing at Foothill College in Los Altos Hills, California, where she also serves as president of MAITRI, a helpline for South Asian women. She is the author of *Arranged Marriage* and *The Mistress of Spices*. She lives with her husband and two children in Sunnyvale, California.

Sujata Bhatt was born in Ahmedabad, India, in 1956, and spent her early years in Pune. She emigrated to the United States in 1968 and received her MFA from the Writers' Workshop, University of Iowa. She now lives in Bremen with her husband and daughter. She has received the Commonwealth Poetry Prize (Asia) for her first book, an Alice Hunt Bartlett Award, and a Cholmondeley Award in 1991. She has four books published by Carcanet: *Brunizem* (1988), *Monkey Shadows* (1991), *The Stinking Rose* (1995) and *Point No Point* (1997).

Dionne Brand was born in Trinidad and has lived in Canada since 1970. She has published two collections of poetry, *No Language is Neutral*, which was shortlisted for the Governor General's Award in

1990, and *Land to Light On* (1997). Her first novel, *In Another Place, Not Here*, was published to critical acclaim in 1996. (The Women's Press, 1997).

Jean 'Binta' Breeze is a poet and performer of international standing. She grew up in rural Jamaica and then lived and worked in Kingston. Coming through on the rhythms and reverberations of reggae, Breeze is known as a 'Dub Poet'. She has performed her work worldwide, including tours of the Caribbean, North America, Europe, South East Asia and Africa. Her writing, recording and theatrical credits include the poetry collections, *Ryddim Ravings* (1988) and *Spring Cleaning* (1992); the script and screenplay of the film *Hallelujah Anyhow*; the direction of the Edgar White play *Moon Dance Night* for the Royal Court Theatre and *In and Out of the Window* for the Black Theatre Cooperative; and the lead in the West End premier of Ntozake Shange's play *The Love Space Demands*. Jean divides her time between Jamaica and London, and has a son and two daughters.

Samantha Coerbell is a New York writer, poet and performer, who has toured the US and Europe with Real LIVE Poetry (formerly known as the Nuyorican Poets Cafe). A Trini-American girl child on an international mission to become an ex-pat, she teaches writing and performance workshops in London, and her poetry has appeared in a number of anthologies. She is currently working on her second self-published collection, and is also writing a screenplay.

Merle Collins is Grenadian. She has studied at the University of the West Indies, Georgetown University in the United States, and at the London School of Economics and Political Science. Her published works include a volume of poems, *Because the Dawn Breaks* (1985), a novel, *Angel* (The Women's Press, 1987), *Watchers and Seekers: Creative Writing by Black Women in Britain* edited with Rhonda Cobham (The Women's Press, 1987), and a volume of short stories, *Rain Darling* (The Women's Press, 1990).

Jayne Cortez was born in Arizona, grew up in California and lives in New York. Her poetry collections include *Mouth on Paper*, *Congratulations* and *Somewhere in Advance of Nowhere*. She has recorded six CDs with her band The Firespitters, including the critically acclaimed *Cheerful and Optimistic*.

Toi Derricote is Professor of English at the University of Pittsburgh, where she teaches courses in creative writing. She is the author of four volumes of poems: *The Empress of the Death House* (1978), *Natural Birth* (1983), *Captivity* (1989), and *Tender* (1998). *The Black Notebooks*, her autobiographical prose, is published by WW Norton.

Rita Dove was born in Akron, Ohio. She was awarded the Pulitzer Prize for poetry in 1987 for *Thomas and Beulah* (1986), in which she recreated the lives of her grandparents from courtship to death. Other collections include *Ten Poems* (1977), *The Yellow House On The Corner* (1980), *Museum* (1983), *The Other Side of the House* (1988), and *Grace Notes* (1989). She has also published a collection of short stories, *Fifth Sunday* (1985); a novel, *Through the Ivory Gate* (1992); and a verse drama, *Darker Face of the Earth* (1994). In 1989 she was appointed Professor of English at the University of Virginia, Charlottesville, and in 1993 she became Commonwealth Professor of English. She was Poet Laureate of the USA from 1993 to 1995.

Ramabai Espinet is a writer and researcher in literature and women studies. She has been active in the women's movement in the Caribbean and Canada. Her essays and her poetry have been published in a number of journals including *CAFRA News*, *Trinidad and Tobago Review*, *Woman Speak* and *Toronto South Asian Review*.

Bernardine Evaristo is the author of the critically acclaimed first poetry collection, *Island of Abraham* (1994) and *Lara*, a verse novel (1997), which was selected as Best of the Year by the *Daily Telegraph*, *New Statesman* and *The Journal*. She was born in London to a Nigerian father and British mother and trained as an actress at the Rose

Bruford College of Speech and Drama. She began her career writing plays which toured England and Europe. Her poetry has been published in numerous anthologies and magazines and she now tours worldwide giving readings of her work.

Honor Ford-Smith is a writer, performer and teacher. She was founding director of the Jamaican theatre company Sistren where she worked until 1989. Her theatre work has been performed throughout the Caribbean and in England, Europe and the United States. Her poems have appeared in several anthologies. Her book with Sistren *Lionheart Gal* was published by The Women's Press in 1986.

Candance L Gardner is a 1998 graduate of Paine College. She was awarded first prize in Papyrus' Writers Showcase Contest Volume 4 for her poem 'she found me'. She currently resides in Nashville, Tennessee.

Nikki Giovanni is one of America's most widely read living poets. She entered the literary world at the height of the Black Arts Movement and quickly achieved not simply fame, but stardom. A recording of her poems became a bestselling album; she has written nearly twenty books, all but one of which are still in print, with several having sold more than a hundred thousand copies. She has been named Woman of the Year by three different magazines, including *Ebony* and is a recipient of a host of honorary doctorates and awards. She has lectured and read from her work at colleges around the United States, and her books include *My House, The Women and the Men, Those Who Ride the Night Winds* and *Sacred Cows*. She is a Professor of English at Virginia Polytechnic.

Lorna Goodison is a major Jamaican poet. Her first book of poems, *Tamarind Season* (1980) was greeted with critical acclaim as was her first public appearance in London in 1985 for the International Poetry Festival and for the Fourth International Book Fair of Radical Black and Third World Books. Her second book of poetry *I am Becoming a Mother* (1986), confirmed her growing reputation and won the Americas section of the British Airways Commonwealth Poetry Prize in 1986.

Amiti Grech was born in Chittagong in undivided India. She is a hillwoman of the Chakma tribe. She has brought out three self-published collections of poetry: *Fifty Poems, Jungle Grass* and *Solitary Crane*, some copies of which are available from the author. She has lived in England for 27 years and has four children and four grandchildren.

Joyoti Grech was born, daughter of Amiti and Tony, in Dhaka, Bangladesh. Her poetry and short stories are published in anthologies, including *Flaming Spirit* (1994), and her plays *Me and Billie Marker* (1995) and *Natural World* (1997) were produced by BBC Radio 4 and Kali Theatre respectively. Her collection of poems, *Travelling Home*, is published by Neruda Press (1998).

Melvina Hazard was born on 2 October, 1971 in Erin, Trinidad and Tobago. Her writing is informed by rage and outrage, not only in herself, but from what she observes of others around her. She is mainly concerned with exposing the injustices she sees and experiences – 'the horrific lagoon monster lurking beneath the bubbly surface of happy island life'. As an afro-indo-amerindo-latino Trinidadian, her work incorporates a 'bastardisation' of several linguistic influences: the 'illiterate' rural dialect, which for her is the strongest vehicle for expressing rage at the mass popular level; the commercialised language of advertising and American cultural imperialism; French/ Spanish patois-colonial baggage; and Creolised Hindi – her lost heritage. Melvina Hazard's poems have appeared in *The Washerwoman Hangs her Poems* and *The Graham House Review*. She has also published INYASPACE, with illustrations by L Mendes, a newspaper series of social, political and personal commentaries; and also the book, INYASPACE. She has been twice awarded the Writer's Union of Trinidad and Tobago Youth Literary Award for Poetry, and also the UNESCO/ASCBERG International Bursaries for the Arts Programme, three month writer's residency with East Midlands Arts, UK.

Safiya Henderson-Holmes is an assistant professor at the Graduate Creative Writing Programme at Syracuse University. She has been published in numerous newsletters and periodicals. Her first collection of poetry, *Madness and a Bit of Hope* won the 1990 William Carlos Williams Award.

bell hooks (Gloria Watkins) grew up in Kentucky. She received her BA at Stanford University and her Ph.D. at the University of California, Santa Cruz. She is now Distinguished Professor of English at City College of New York. bell hooks received the Before Columbus Foundation's 1991 American Book Award for *Yearning: Race, Gender and Cultural Politics.* In 1990, The American Studies Critic's Choice Panel chose *Talking Back* as one of the most outstanding recent books in the area of Education Studies. Her poetry collection *A Woman's Mourning Song* was published in 1993 and her works of memoir, *Bone Black: Memories of Girlhood* (1997) and *Wounds of Passion: A Writing Life* (1998) are both published by The Women's Press.

Allison Joseph was born in London and is an Assistant Professor of creative writing and literature at Southern Illinois University. Her poems have appeared in numerous periodicals including *The Kenyon Review, Parnassus and Callaloo.* She is the author of *What Keeps Us Here* (1992), a volume of poems. She graduated from Kenyon College and received the MFA from Indiana University.

Ka'Frique aka Khefri Riley is a founding member of the Urban Poets Society where she helped establish a young, black British performance poetry scene. Producer and Co-Artistic Director of Mannafest, she has produced and promoted several theatrical, musical, innovative events involving collaborations and fusions between art forms. Performing under the stage name of Ka'Frique she has shared the spotlight with The Last Poets, Steve Williamson and Michael Franti of Spearhead. She is featured on several poetry compilation albums, including *Tongue & Groove & Chocolate Art* in London and *Amber Records* in Germany and *UFO* in Japan.

Parm Kaur has been writing poetry for ten years. She has performed as a solo artist and in collaboration with dancers and musicians at a variety of national and international venues, including the Barbican Centre and ICA, London, the Kronberg, Copenhagen, and the Hypotheses in Oaxaca, Mexico. She has appeared on Channel 4's *The Big Breakfast* and her poems have been broadcast on BBC Radio, including Radio 4's *Woman's Hour*. She has been published in a number of poetry journals and magazines.

Jackie Kay was born in Scotland in 1961. Her first collection, *The Adoption Papers* was published by Bloodaxe in 1991. It received a Scottish Arts Council Book Award, a Saltire First Book of the Year Award and a Forward Prize in 1992, and was also shortlisted for the *Mail on Sunday*/John Llewellyn Rhys Prize. Her book of poetry for children, *Two's Company* (1992) won the Signal Poetry Award in 1993. Jackie Kay has written widely for stage and television. She lives in London.

Shamshad Khan was conceived in Karachi and born in Britain. She lives in Manchester and works for the Greater Manchester Low Pay Unit. She is literature adviser to North West Arts Board and co-editor of Commonword's Northern Black Women's poetry anthology. Her short story 'The Woman and the Chair' was published in 1994 and her poetry appears in a number of anthologies. Shamshad Khan has had her work broadcast on local and national radio. She has performed her poetry using soundtracks and working with contemporary dancers.

Rosamond S King is a poet and scholar who does development work in the non-profit sector. Her poetry has been published in journals such as *Poet Lore, Obsidian II, Another Chicago Magazine* and *The Caribbean Writer*. She works or has worked with the groups Colored Women Colored Wor(l)ds, No 1 Gold Artists' Collective and BlaWoWoW (Black Women Who Write).

Janet Kofi-Tsekpo was born in Portsmouth, England to a Ghanaian father and British mother. Educated at the University of Manchester and at the School of Oriental and African Studies, University of London, she received an MA in Area Studies, Africa, and was winner of the Zeena Ralph Memorial Prize for her essay, 'Healing the wounds: interpretations of identity and "race"' (1996). She has worked in publishing, youth work, theatre and education, and currently does research for an arts consultancy. She lives and works in London.

Amy Ling was born in Beijing, China and emigrated at age six to the US with her parents and younger brother. She has lived in the United States, Mexico and France, and presently resides in Washington DC with her husband and two children. She has a Ph.D. in Comparative Literature from New York University and has taught at Georgetown University and Harvard. Jolted by the civil rights and women's movements into the realisation that her own between-worlds history was worthy of literary exploration and research, she wrote these deeply personal poems, which appear in *Chinamerican Reflections* (1984).

Stacy Makishi is a performance artist/poet who resides in Hackney, London, which is the subject of her new mixed-media project called 'On The Street Where I Live', funded by the London Arts Board. Her solo show, 'Tongue in Sheets' was commissioned by Dixon Place NYC. Current work also includes a collaboration with Split Britches Theatre Company on a show called 'The Salad of the Bad Cafe'. She is the recipient of the Franklin Furnace Award for her new show 'Runt' which will be broadcast live over the Internet.

Rachel Manley. Born in Cornwall of an English mother and a Jamaican father, Rachel Manley came to Jamaica at the age of two. She grew up with her grandparents, N W Manley, intellectual shaper and leader of Jamaica's nationalist movement, and Edna Manley, the sculptor and promoter of Jamaican arts. Her father a trade unionist and politician, she was involved in a life which was 'tumultuous and inspiring, rooted in the spirit of Jamaica'. She is the author of two previous collections of poetry, *Prisms* and *Poems 2* and the editor of *Edna Manley: The Diaries*. She has two sons and lives in Canada.

Laureen Mar received her BA in English from the University of Washington in 1975, and her MFA in Creative Writing from Columbia University in 1979. She was the Program Associate for Poets' and Writers' Group and the Public Information Director of the New York State Council for the Arts. She returned to Seattle, Washington, in 1986 and became Public Relations Coordinator of the Seattle Arts Museum and lecturer in Asian American Poetry at the University of Washington. Laureen Mar's poetical works have appeared in many magazines and anthologies.

Dana Marrett-Silvera is of Jamaican parentage and was born in the UK. She is a writer, social work manager, counsellor and trainer, and has worked in England and the Caribbean. Her writing has been, and continues to be, a stimulating and often revealing expression of her experiences, feelings, fears and imagination. She has run creative-writing workshops, facilitated black women's writing groups in Sheffield and has used writing as a counselling tool. 'Silent Talking' is her first published poem.

Hope Massiah is a Barbados-born, London-bred writer and management consultant. She has discovered that being a dreamy poet one day, and a linear, analytical report writer the next, is character building. Her story '1985' appeared in *Does Your Mama Know? An Anthology of Black Lesbian Coming Out Stories* (1997).

Kamilah Aisha Moon is a writer, poet and performance artist and has self-published three volumes of poetry, *Love Changes, Vision at Sunset and Other Poems* (1995), and *Phat Gyrl Verse: A Young Life Revisited* (1997). She is active as both a performer and organiser on the reading and performance circuit, and she performed and co-ordinated the Harlem Renaissance poetry reading at the Morris Museum in Augusta, Georgia. She is a member of the writers' group The Inkwell Collective.

Raman Mundair was born in Panjab, India, but was raised in Manchester and Leicestershire, England. She is a writer of prose and poetry, a playwright and a screenwriter. She is also a singer and creativity workshop facilitator. Her work as a poet is anthologised in *The Fire People* and *The Memorybird* and has been featured on BBC Radio 4's *Woman's Hour*, BBC World Service and Channel 4 television. As a playwright her work has been staged at Interplay Europe Festival 98, Berlin, the West Yorkshire Playhouse, Leeds and the Institute of Contemporary Arts, London. At present she is developing stage plays for Talawa and Tamasha Theatre Companies and 'Objects of Desire' a short film for Sankofa Film Company.

Grace Nichols was born and educated in Georgetown, Guyana, but has lived in Britain since 1977, where she now works as a freelance writer. In 1983 she won the Commonwealth Poetry Prize with her first book of poems: *i is a long-memoried woman*. Her other work includes *The Fat Black Woman's Poems* (1984), *Lazy Thoughts of a Lazy Woman* (1989) and her first novel, *Whole of a Morning Sky* (1986). Her books for children include two collections of short stories, two books of poems, *Come On Into My Tropical Garden* (1988), and *Give Yourself a Hug* (1994); and anthologies such as: *Poetry Jump Up, Can't Buy a Slice of Sky?* and *A Caribbean Dozen*. Grace Nichols lives in Sussex with her family.

Pat Parker was born in Houston, Texas in 1944 and wrote since she was a child. From making greeting cards 'for festive occasions', to becoming the first woman editor of her high school newspaper, to changing majors (and schools) from journalism to creative writing after the head of journalism insisted 'there's no place for blacks in this field', the author understood the power and pleasure of the word – written and spoken. Pat Parker – black lesbian poet, feminist medical administrator, mother of two daughters, softball devotee and general progressive troublemaker – died of breast cancer in 1989 at the age of forty-five.

Vanessa Richards is a London-based and Vancouver-born, poet, performer, workshop facilitator and 'student of the word'. Canada's underground music and experimental art scene in the 1980s nurtured the artist. She has performed in North America, and the Caribbean and her writing has featured in magazines and anthologies, and on recordings. Vanessa Richards is a founder and Artistic Director of Mannafest, a performance poetry company.

Olive Senior has worked as Editor of the *Jamaica Journal* and *Social and Economic Studies*. Her collection of short stories, *Summer Lightning*, won the Commonwealth Writers' Prize in 1987. Her other publications include *A–Z of Jamaican Heritage*, *The Message is Change*, *Talking of Trees*, *The Arrival of the Snake Woman* and *Gardening in the Tropics* (1994/5).

Ntozake Shange is the author of the Obie Award winning 'For Colored Girls Who Have Considered Suicide/When the Rainbow is Enuf', 'A Photograph: Lovers-in-Motion', 'Spell # 7', 'Boogie, Woogie Landscapes', and an adaptation of *Educating Rita*. She has also written several novels, including *Sassafras, Cypress & Inigo*, *Betsey Brown* and *Liliane: Resurrection of the Daughter*, and is currently working on her new novel *Some Sing, Some Cry*. Ntozake Shange is Associate Professor of Drama and English at Prairie View A&M University in Texas where she is also a member of the Texas Institute of Letters. She has received numerous awards including a National Endowment for the Arts Fellowship, a Guggenheim Fellowship, The Medal of Excellence from Columbia University, The Distinguished Medal of Achievement from Barnard College, and the City of Philadelphia Artist's Award. Ntozake Shange was named 'A Living Legend in Black Theatre' by the National Black Theatre Festival in 1995, and Heavyweight Poetry Champion of the World 1992–4.

Dorothea Smartt is a poet and live artist, born in England, raised by Bajan parents. She was an Institute of Contemporary Arts, Attached Live Artist (1995–6). She reads and performs in Britain and abroad, and has been awarded several commissions and bursaries. Her poetry appears in various anthologies, most recently *Mythic Women/Real Women* (1998) and *The Fire People* (1998). She is Co-editor of *Words from the Women's Cafe* (1993). She recently received an Arts Council of England award to develop a new work *MedusaPlay* and is hoping to publish her first collection of poetry. She lectures part-time at Birkbeck College and the University of Leeds.

Sharan Strange is a native of Orangeburg, South Carolina. She was educated at Harvard College and received the MFA in Poetry from Sarah Lawrence College. Her work has been published in numerous journals and anthologies, including *Agni, American Poetry Review, Callaloo, The Garden Thrives: Twentieth Century African-American Poetry* and *Best American Poetry,* and she has exhibited at the Institute of Contemporary Art in Boston and the Whitney Museum in New York. She currently lives in Washington, DC where she teaches writing, literature and social studies in an alternative high school.

Zebbie Todd has been writing poetry and stories from a young age. Born in England of Jamaican immigrants, she is a single parent with four children. She is a qualified child development agent, youth worker and a teacher. Currently she is working on her Ph.D. in parapsychology. She is also a workshop facilitator and stress management consultant.

Alice Walker was born in Eatonton, Georgia. She has received many awards, including the Radcliffe Institute medal and a Guggenheim Fellowship. Her hugely popular novel *The Color Purple* won the American Book Award and the Pulitzer Prize for Fiction in 1983 and was subsequently made into an internationally successful film by Steven Spielberg. Alice Walker's other novels include *The Temple of My Familiar,* a *New York Times* bestseller; *The Third Life of Grange Copeland; Meridan; Possessing the Secret of Joy* and *By the Light of My Father's Smile.* She has written two collections of short stories, *In Love and Trouble* and *You Can't Keep a Good Woman Down;* and three books of essays and memoirs, *Anything We Love Can Be Saved: A Writer's Activism; In Search of our Mothers' Gardens: Womanist Prose*; and *Living by the Word*. Alice Walker has published four books of poetry: *Horses Make a Landscape Look More Beautiful; Once, Revolutionary Petunias*; and *Goodnight, Willie Lee, I'll See You in the Morning*. Her complete poetry is now collected, in one volume, *Her Blue Body, Everything We Know: Earthling Poems 1965–1990 Complete*, and her complete short stories appear in *The Complete Stories*. She is also the co-author with Pratibha Parmar of the film and book *Warrior Marks*; and her memoir, *The Same River Twice: Honoring the Difficult* was published in 1996.

Akure Wall was born in Lagos to a Nigerian mother and an English father. At six her family moved to Croydon. Growing up listening to a mix of 'punk, hi-life, disco and rap', Akure began writing as a way of exploring her own life and its contradictions. After living in New York for seven years, Akure became involved with a performnance poetry collective called Urban Poets' Society in London, and performed extensively in venues such as the ICA, the Royal Festival Hall and festivals in Barcelona, Germany and New York. She also set up a publishing company, One Inc, producing a book of performance pieces, *Croydon Soul Patrol*, and is currently writing an album of soundscapes – word based collaborations – with various musicians.

Lamia Ben Youssef is a doctoral student in the English Department at Michigan State University. She taught American Literature at the University of Tunis for three years, and in May 1995 she received a Fulbright Scholarship from AMIDEAST which allowed her to resume her doctoral studies in African-American women writers, feminist theory and criticism, and post-colonial literature at Michigan State.

S Lee Yung received her BA in Western Art History at Hunter College, New York. She has been the Treasurer, General Administrator and Artist in Residence of Basement Workshop. Her poetry has appeared in many magazines and anthologies including *Bridge, Contact 2,* and others. She was the co-editor of *American Born* *and Foreign: An Anthology of Asian American Poetry*, published by the poetry magazine *Sudbury*. Her interests are wide-ranging, including Caribbean conga drumming and Arnis Philippine stick fighting.

Permissions Acknowledgements

Grateful thanks and acknowledgement are given to the following authors and copyright holders for permission to reproduce poems from material in copyright.

Patience Agbabi for 'Sentences', *R.A.W.*, Patience Agbabi, Gecko Press, 1995; and 'Ajax' which appears in *The Fire People*, Payback Press, 1998.

Virago Press for 'Woman at Work' and 'Phenomenal Woman', *Maya Angelou: The Complete Collected Poems*, Virago, 1995; 'Mother ...Sister...Daughter', *Spring Cleaning*, Jean 'Binta' Breeze', Virago, 1992; 'The Sheep and the Goats', *Rotten Pomerack*, Merle Collins, Virago, 1992; 'Why Shouldn't She' by Grace Nichols from *The Fat Black Woman's Poems*, Virago, 1984.

Chitra Banarjee Divakaruni, Sandra Dijkstra Literary Agency, for 'The Nishi' and from 'Learning to Dance', from *Leaving Yuba City*, by Chitra Banarjee Divakaruni. Copyright © 1997 by Chitra Banarjee Divakaruni. Used by permission of Doubleday, a division of Bantam Doubleday Dell Publishing Group, Inc.

Carcanet Press Ltd for 'Frauenjournal', *The Stinking Rose*, Sujata Bhatt, Carcanet Press Ltd, 1995; 'Swami Anand', and (Udaylee) from *Brunizem*, Sujata Bhatt, Carcanet Press, 1988.

'Land to Light On' from *Land to Light On* by Dionne Brand; 'Hurricane Story, 1988' and 'Plants', from *Gardening in the Tropics*, Olive Senior. Used by permission, McClelland & Stewart, Inc. The Canadian Publishers.

Curtis Brown Group Ltd for 'Hoping' from *Red Petticoat* and 'The Sheep and the Goats' from *Rotten Pomerack*, Virago Press, 1992.

Serpent's Tail for 'Global Inequalities' and 'Samba is Power', *Somewhere in Advance of Nowhere*, Jayne Cortez, High Risk Books, Serpent's Tail, 1996. Reprinted by permission of Serpent's Tail, London

Bloodaxe Books for 'Some of My Worst Wounds', *Heartease*, Lorna Goodison, Bloodaxe Books, 1988; 'In my country', 'Keeping Orchids' and 'Other Lovers', *Other Lovers*, Jackie Kay, Bloodaxe Books, 1993.

W W Norton & Company for 'Particulars' fom *Grace Notes*, Copyright © 1989 by Rita Dove. Reprinted by permission of the author and W W Norton & Company, Inc. Rita Dove 'The Bistro Styx', from *Mother Love*, by Rita Dove. Copyright © 1995.

Sister Vision Press: Copyright © Espinet, Ramabai, 'Afterbirth' and 'City Blues' from *Nuclear Seasons*, Ramabai Espinet, Sister Vision Press, 1991; Copyright © Ford-Smith, Honor, 'Dinner at the Apartment in Toronto' from *My Mother's Last Dance*, SisterVision Press, 1996.

Angela Royal Publishing for 'An Abridged Excerpt from *Lara*', *Lara*, Bernardine Evaristo, Angela Royal Publishing, 1997.

William Morrow & Co Inc for 'I Laughed When I Wrote It' from *My House* by Nikki Giovanni, © 1972 by Nikki Giovanni. By permission of William Morrow & Company, Inc.

New Beacon Books for 'Tightrope Walker', *I Am Becoming My Mother*, Lorna Goodison, New Beacon Books,1986.

Writers and Readers Publishing Inc for 'A Girl and Her Doll', *Daily Bread*, Safiya Henderson-Holmes, Harlem River Press; 'they warmakers', *A Woman's Mourning Song*, bell hooks, Harlem River Press, 1990.

'On Sidewalks, On Streetcorners, As Girls' from *In Every Seam*, by Allison Joseph, © 1997. Reprinted by permission of the University of Pittsburgh Press.

Peepal Tree Press Ltd for 'Memoryectomy', *A Light Left On*, Rachel Manley, Peepal Tree Press, 1992.

244

Index of Poets

Index of Poems

Index of First Lines

The Women's Press is Britain's leading women's publishing house. Established in 1978, we publish high-quality fiction and non-fiction from outstanding women writers worldwide. Our exciting and diverse list includes literary fiction, detective novels, biography and autobiography, health, women's studies, handbooks, literary criticism, psychology and self-help, the arts, our popular Livewire Books series for young women and the bestselling annual Women Artists Diary featuring beautiful colour and black-and-white illustrations from the best in contemporary women's art.

If you would like more information about our books or about our mail order book club, please send an A5 sae for our latest catalogue and complete list to:

The Sales Department
The Women's Press Ltd
34 Great Sutton Street
London EC1V 0DX
Tel: 0171 251 3007
Fax: 0171 608 1938